Trumpet Call to Prayer

Trumpet Call to Prayer

Raymond Borlase

The quotations from the scriptures
are taken from the New American
Standard Version, unless otherwise stated.

Marshall Morgan and Scott
Life Changing Books
Marshall Pickering
3 Beggarwood Lane, Basingstoke, Hants RG23 7LP, UK

Copyright © 1986 by Raymond Borlase

First published in 1986 by Marshall Morgan
and Scott Publications Ltd
Part of the Marshall Pickering Holdings Group
A subsidiary of the Zondervan Corporation

British Library Cataloguing in Publication Data

Borlase, Raymond
   Trumpet Call to Prayer.
   1. Prayer
   I. Title
   248.3'2   BV210.2

   ISBN 0-551-01399-0

Typeset by Input Typesetting Ltd, London SW19 8DR
Printed and bound in Great Britain

Contents

Acknowledgements

I am profoundly grateful to many brothers and sisters in Christ who have shaped my ministry by their witness, teaching, encouragement and correction. This book is a token of my appreciation of the late Denis Clark whose inspired ministry not only taught me so much from the Word of God, but also about spiritual warfare. I am thankful to God that I ever came under his ministry. Alex Buchanan first introduced me to Prayer and Bible Weeks and Intercessors for Britain, and hence to the ministry of Denis Clark. Alex was also a help and inspiration particularly in those early days of learning to walk in the Spirit.

I want to express also my thanks to those who have helped me with the manuscript by reading, correcting, and making helpful suggestions.

I am indebted to each member of Moreton Christian Fellowship. For seventeen years, they have supported me and have encouraged me especially as God has taken me into a wider ministry. They have been willing to relinquish their pastor increasingly as the work of IFB has expanded. I thank God for their love and care which has grown over the years into a deep bond of trust and fellowship in Christ.

Finally I pay tribute to my wife and family. The older boys have helped to run off copies of the manuscript on the computer print-out. All through my ministry, however, my wife has provided the secure base from which I operate. She has never complained about trips abroad, or the many lonely evenings when a pastor has to be about kingdom business. I therefore record my thanks to God for her love, support and encouragement.

Preface

During the early part of 1985, I was asked to write a book on prayer. At that stage, I declined for a number of reasons, not least that I felt no confirmation from the Lord. During the late summer, I received a second invitation from another publisher, and began to wonder whether it might be right after all. By that time, I had been asked by the trustees of Intercessors For Britain to take on the leadership of IFB in succession to Alex Buchanan. I, therefore, began to feel that perhaps this approach to write a book was timely and wondered whether it was from God. A few days later I was reading in Exodus 17:14, 'Write this in a book as a memorial, and recite it to Joshua, that I will utterly blot out the memory of Amalek from under heaven.' That command from God to Moses was given after the battle between the Israelites and Amalekites. During that conflict Moses had lifted up his hands in prayer and as a result Israel won a notable victory. I felt that God wanted me to put on record some of the battles we have fought in prayer both within IFB (Intercessors For Britain) and my own church, Moreton Christian Fellowship. My having prayed over the matter, it seemed right to record these details, not simply as a memorial, but as a means of teaching and encouraging God's people to engage in spiritual warfare.

I believe it is also essential to say here that although the following chapters record some amazing answers to our prayers, in no way are we claiming that *we* achieved those results. In the first place, it is only God who acts. Although

He wants our co-operation, and even invests in us His authority; we cannot go beyond His will, or make the slightest change to a situation without His gracious hand. Therefore, I want to make it clear that on every occasion of answered prayer, we give God the glory and rejoice that He hears our prayers. The glory is His alone.

Secondly, although these particular incidents have been our experiences, I believe others throughout the country have often prayed in a similar way and we rejoice that we have been part of a great army that has fought against the forces of darkness, and pleaded with Almighty God. We have discovered frequently that we have been united with many Christians in praying for specific needs. We are all under the leading of the same Holy Spirit who aids and directs our praying. Inevitably, these events can only be presented as our personal testimony, but I trust that many others will see a reflection of their own prayer battles in our story and will be encouraged in their spiritual warfare.

Finally, my ultimate aim in recording our prayer experiences is to set out some clear teaching on the various aspects of prayer, intercession and spiritual warfare. This book is therefore dedicated to that end. I present it to the Body of Christ with the express desire and fervent prayer that the people of God will pray for their nation as never before, and that God will move by His mighty power throughout the world. I believe that, like the Israelites under Joshua, we need to possess our land for God.

1

Tell Father!

As new born babes in Christ our first cry, when we receive the Spirit of adoption, is 'Abba Father' (see Romans 8.15). I'll never forget the first time I heard that actual Hebrew word. I was sitting by the Dead Sea in Israel when I heard a little lad calling out to his father, 'Abba, Abba.' His words sounded so full of warmth and excitement. As they continued to echo in my ears, I was thrilled to think that I had the same sort of relationship with my Heavenly Father and could come to him in the same way. It might seem a little irreverent to address God as 'Daddy', but that's the closeness and warmth of relationship that God wants us to know and experience.

Scripture is full of this concept of God as our Father. John records Jesus talking about God as 'Father' or 'My Father' on ninety-nine occasions! Sometimes, Jesus addressed God in prayer as 'Holy Father', and on other occasions as 'Abba Father' (Mark 14:36). He taught us to call God 'Our Father.' I don't think we fully appreciate the joy of a relationship with a Father who really cares and loves His children.

When I've been away from home for a while, it is one of my greatest delights, on my return, to see the children rush to the door and hear them cry, 'Daddy, Daddy.' In a moment, I'm surrounded by four very excited children all wanting to give me a hug. It's not very long before Ruth, who is five, is undoing my case to see what goodies I have brought home this time. It reminds me of the Scripture: 'If you being evil, know how to give good gifts to your children, how much more shall your Father who is in heaven give what is good to those who ask Him.' (Matthew 7:11). David, our youngest, gives me such a big hug that I'm in danger of suffocating! Jason is soon telling me all that he has done, which may include news of his latest swimming certificate. Mark, the oldest, sometimes needs drawing out a little, but they all want to tell me what has been happening.

That's the delight of family life. God wants us to enjoy that sort of relationship with Him, and for it to be as warm, loving, and natural as a good father-child relationship should be. God is the perfect Father, so we should be able to delight in our fellowship with Him.

There are times when my wife has to prompt our children. Perhaps in the excitement they have forgotten some vital piece of news, so Val says, 'Tell Daddy about . . .' Other times she has to remind them to break some less pleasant news: 'Tell Daddy what you've broken,' she says. Eventually the confession comes, perhaps a little tearfully, yet the information is shared.

It seems to me that there are times when the Holy Spirit gently whispers, 'Tell Father.' It may be something that needs to be prayed through, whether good or bad. At other times, the Spirit prompts us to confess our sins, so that our relationship may not be impaired and that we might receive God's forgiveness.

Another thing that I appreciate about our family life is all that we can enjoy together on holiday. There are times when we have all joined in a game of football or cricket; watched aircraft at busy and noisy airports; explored the hidden depths of rock pools, dived into the surf of the sea, or even made sand castles. It's the joy of sharing life together that is so good. Part of the delight of knowing God is to be able to share the beauty of a sunset or a mountain scene, and say, 'Father, You have created a beautiful world.'

There are occasions, when as a father, I need to recognise the weaknesses of my children. David can't do up his shoe-laces yet, but to insist that he should do so would be cruel, and, to say the least, lacking in understanding. Yet some people's concept of God is of that nature; they see Him as a cruel God who demands perfection and the impossible. Scripture says, however, 'As a father has compassion on his children, so the Lord has compassion on those who fear Him. For He Himself knows our frame; He is mindful that we are but dust' (Psalm 103:13,14). We can come to God in prayer knowing that He appreciates our weaknesses and is ready to help us in our struggles.

The trouble with some Christians is that they equate God with their own father who may have been cruel, unjust or even depraved. They see God as a copy of their father, instead of realising that he is a very bad copy of God, the Father. Paul puts it this way: 'I bow my knees before the Father, from whom every family in heaven and on earth derives its name . . .' (Ephesians 3:14,15). My fatherhood is derived from God, not the other way around. Jesus showed that at best I am evil, although giving good gifts to my children, but the true Father in heaven gives, in far greater measure, what is for our good, including the Holy Spirit (see Luke 11:13).

John in his first letter says: 'I have written to you little children, because you know the Father' (1 John 2:13). I believe that here, John is addressing new-born babes in Christ, and expressing the wonder of their sonship in having the joy of really knowing Father. If we add to that Paul talking about bowing the knee to Father in prayer; Jesus not only talking about Father, but praying to 'Abba Father' and teaching us to pray 'Our Father'; and then remember that the Holy Spirit brings about the cry of 'Abba' at the moment of new birth, we have a most impressive picture of prayer as talking to Father. It is as if Father, Son and Holy Spirit all want us to share in the sheer wonder, warmth and joy of talking to God as our perfect heavenly Father.

Prayer is telling Father about our joys and sorrows, our hopes and fears, our perplexities and anxieties. If we formalise prayer, we destroy it because it should be an expression of our feelings to God. If we neglect it, we lose

13

a loving relationship that is vital to our well-being. We need to tell Father.

Just as a child feels free to express his feelings to a father, so we need to tell our heavenly Father how we feel. If my children have been beaten up on the way home, or have been treated unfairly at school, they don't come with beautiful polished phrases, but they pour out their hearts and their hurts. There is the same degree of realism in the Psalms. David says, 'Pour out your heart before Him; God is a refuge for us' (Psalm 62:8).

David didn't just teach these things, but practised them, for he writes: 'I cry aloud with my voice to the Lord; I make supplication with my voice to the Lord. I pour out my complaint before Him; I declare my trouble before Him' (Psalm 142:1,2). Yet the psalm that most impresses me was written in the middle of a civil war when his own son, Absalom, had sought to seize the throne. David had been forced to leave his own home and the security of Jerusalem to the cries and curses of Shimei. In the psalm he relates how his adversaries had increased and were saying there was no hope for him. Then he continues: 'But You, O Lord, are a shield about me; my glory, and the One who lifts my head. I was crying to the Lord with my voice, and He answered me from His holy mountain.' An incredible statement follows: 'I lay down and slept' (Psalm 3:5). David didn't suffer from insomnia, even in the middle of a civil war, because he had poured out his heart to God and been comforted.

The chapters that follow in this book will consider matters such as intercession, spiritual warfare and revival, but it seems to me that until we have grasped the simple concept that prayer is telling Father, and delight in talking with Him, then prayer, at best, will only be a religious duty, and not the thrill of a warm relationship. The beginning of prayer is knowing Abba, Father.

2

The Making of an Intercessor

I can remember very clearly, how, while I was still in my teens, our whole family was thrown into disarray. My younger brother was rushed into hospital with acute earache. It wasn't altogether unusual for him to suffer in this way, but this had seemed far more serious. Eventually the diagnosis was given that Keith was suffering from a mastoid and would need an operation. I recall our pastor calling at our home and praying for my brother. Special prayer was made for him at the Church prayer meeting that was held on a Friday evening at 10 o'clock. As a mastoid operation was at that time considered to be a very serious and dangerous matter, strong prayer was made on my brother's behalf that God would heal him.

Two days after the prayer meeting, my parents visited my brother in hospital. He greeted them with the news that he could go home. My parents were very sceptical about this and felt sure that Keith had been mistaken. They imagined that it was more likely he was going to be transferred to another ward or even another hospital. When they made enquiries from the ward sister, they discovered that to everyone's amazement the mastoid had completely disappeared. God had powerfully intervened.

On another occasion, Keith had been badly burnt on the backs of his legs. A chip pan had caught fire, and as my father rushed outside with the pan, he had accidentally spilt some of the burning fat over Keith. The specialist at the hospital considered that it would be necessary for Keith to have a skin graft. We, as a family, prayed that God would heal my brother's legs. Little by little the legs began to heal until the day came when the specialist stated that a skin graft would not be necessary. Keith let out an involuntary, 'Praise the Lord!'

During these events, I was learning, as a young Christian, something about prayer that challenged my understanding and commitment to pray to God. I had been brought up in a church that believed in prayer. The 10 o'clock prayer meeting held on a Friday night had begun some years earlier, at the time when Col. Mary Booth was to speak at our Church. She was the then sole surviving daughter of the founder of the Salvation Army. The prayer meeting had been arranged, at Mary Booth's request, to pray that people would be saved the following Sunday. I can remember now many people going forward to the front of the Church to receive Jesus as their Saviour that night. Among them was a tall national service sailor who went forward, breaking his heart as he sought the Lord.

The Friday night prayer meeting continued, and so did the blessing. For nearly six months after Col. Mary Booth's visit, people were being saved week by week. On one Sunday evening over twenty people responded to an appeal at a baptismal service. The chairman of the Evangelism Committee of the Southern Baptist Association described those 6 months as a mini-revival. They were amazing days as God's Spirit touched many lives.

By the time I had left the Northern Grammar School, and begun an apprenticeship, at the age of 18 in Portsmouth Dockyard, I had started to attend those Friday night prayer meetings. Those revival scenes had mostly gone but we continued to pray for God's blessing. I believe that God was doing something in me at that time. My prayer-life was being shaped and encouraged. It was something of a sacrifice to pray from 10 o'clock to around midnight and then have to cycle along 4 miles of mainly unlit roads to the outskirts of Portsmouth where I lived. I was, however, learning something vital about prayer and a prayer-answering God.

If those days in Tangier Road Baptist Church were being

used to shape an intercessor, other factors were to be at work which would dim the vision. I spent four years in theological training for the ministry. While it was a good evangelical college, we had to study subjects like philosophy which had a subtle effect on me. One of the concepts of philosophy was that in a rational universe, there could be no such thing as a miracle, for that would break the laws of the universe. Whilst I rejected such ideas, a seed had been sown that brought a harvest of doubt. Subconsciously my acceptance of the infallibility of the Word of God was weakened, as was faith in a God of miracles. The phrase, 'Thy will be done' became a nice escape clause to add onto the end of a prayer in case there was no answer.

In spite of this, I began to read, along with other Baptist ministers in Luton, about the ministry of healing. Our search, however, broadened out into enquiring about the gifts of the Holy Spirit. It brought us into contact with others from other denominations who were experiencing the baptism of the Holy Spirit. The charismatic movement was already beginning to affect church life in Britain in the 60's, but it was not until 1971, after I had moved to Merseyside, that I was finally filled with the Spirit.

This had an immediate effect upon me, for the Word of God became a living Book. I suddenly found a new understanding of God's word, which four years in theological college had not brought. It now became a delight to meet with God in prayer. It was no longer just a Christian duty which had to be fulfilled for the sake of my Christian life; it was now a delight talking to Father, and knowing that He cared for me. It had all been so intellectual before. Of course, I accepted that God knew all about me and our church; after all, that was one of His divine attributes. What a revelation, however, when such knowledge touched my heart, and to know that all I was experiencing touched His heart. He knew my disappointments and heartbreaks in the ministry and felt these things Himself. Now I knew that I could have a meaningful conversation with Him in prayer concerning the pastorate and the people. I could pray with a new urgency and expect God to work. Soon

17

God began to renew others and change the Church. It was soon after this that we began to experience the first resistance to the work of the Spirit. It then became even more important to seek God's guidance in these uncharted waters, and to know His comforting hand.

It was around this time that a friend of mine invited me to a Prayer and Bible Week under the leadership of Denis Clark. At the beginning of 1969 he had founded Intercessors For Britain and now, four years later, the first Prayer and Bible Week was being held. During that week God met with me in a powerful way that was to change my ministry completely. Firstly, God showed me how unbalanced my ministry was. My concept of God's love lacked the balance of His discipline and judgement. God then showed me that so much of my ministry was that of seeking to please men rather than God. At the heart of it all was the fear of men. I knew from that point onwards I could only seek to please God. That was pretty revolutionary as far as my ministry was concerned.

There was, however, another aspect to that week which I had never come across before. We began praying about the government, trade unions, pornography, and, of course, the Church. At the same time we were waging war against the principalities and powers that were dominating these situations and our national life. Much of this was completely new to me. To expect God to answer specific prayers on national matters and also to rebuke the powers of darkness was a completely different concept of prayer. What was more, to see answers in these matters during the course of the week was amazing. I saw for the first time the need to concentrate prayer on specific matters rather than hopping around the world from one subject to another. If we were to destroy the strongholds of Satan, it would only be by sustained attacks in prayer.

About the same time, I began to read the book '*Intercessor*' which is the story of Rees Howells and how God led him in intercession. I was thrilled and challenged to see how God led him and those with him, at the Bible College of Wales, during the war years. Again and again as they prayed about the various nations, they felt God directed their prayers according to His purposes concerning those nations. They were aware of God's mercy towards Britain as they sought Him to spare us from a Nazi invasion and to destroy that evil regime.

We slowly began within our own Church to pray about national issues and see that there was a spiritual battle to be fought. It wasn't easy at first, for we tended to pray around in circles rather than concentrate on specific targets. Slowly over the years, however, we made progress. Many of our fellowship are now committed to pray for at least one hour a week for our nation, and are linked with Intercessors For Britain. As a Church we have seen some tremendous answers to prayer, some of which are shared in this book. It is always good to see a Church move into strong intercession and spiritual warfare. Yet perhaps, more than anything else, I am aware that God's hand has been gently leading me on more deeply into intercession. It is not a work that I have sought because it is arduous and costly, but I know that my life has been shaped by the Father's loving hand. Yet, for all this, one is constantly aware that there is still much to learn. All I know is that God has called me to this work and it is a privilege to learn from Jesus, the Great Intercessor, something more of this ministry. Paul's words are a tremendous encouragement to me: 'Faithful is He who calls you, and He also will bring it to pass' (1 Thessalonians 5:24).

3

A Royal Priesthood

Within Christianity today, there is much rejoicing that we are a royal priesthood. It is a tremendous delight to know that we have been called into royal service. We rejoice that we can offer up 'spiritual sacrifices' to God (1 Peter 2:5) and we bring our praise and worship with much joy, but we are sometimes slow to recognise that part of the priestly function is that of intercession. David in appointing the Levites to minister before the ark, instructed them 'to make petition, to give thanks, and to praise the Lord, the God of Israel' (1 Chronicles 16:4, NIV). The writer to the Hebrews reminds us that because the priestly ministry of Jesus is permanent, 'He always lives to make intercession for us' (Hebrews 7:25). Being a part of a royal priesthood then requires us to plead with God, on behalf of others, before the throne of grace. It is that aspect of the priestly ministry that is frequently missing today.

The Old Testament ritual of anointing the priests has some very significant lessons for those who would seek to enter into this ministry. This is illustrated very clearly in Leviticus 8 where Aaron and his sons are anointed as priests.

The first act of their consecration was that they were washed with water (v 6). Before we can begin to pray on behalf of others we need first to be cleansed. Paul in Titus 3:5 talks about the 'washing of regeneration'. He makes it plain that we are not saved through our own acts of righteousness, but through a new birth experience by the Holy Spirit. The beginning of the new life is expressed in baptism as the believer is symbolically buried and raised to enter a new life. Without being born again we cannot enter the kingdom of God, and cannot consequently be part of a royal priesthood.

We shall see later that some of the blood from the ram of ordination was also applied to the priest. This emphasises that the cleansing is through the blood of Christ. This is made very clear by John, who states, 'He (Jesus) released us from our sins by His blood, and He has made us to be a kingdom, priests to our God and Father' (Revelation 1:5,6). The cleansing that we receive by faith in Christ is absolutely vital if we are to lift up holy hands in prayer as Paul urges us to do in 1 Timothy 2:8. That will involve not only that initial cleansing in Christ when we are first saved, but making sure that we are being cleansed from sin as we come to pray to a Holy God.

Secondly, the priest had various items of clothing placed on him. The major items were the robe, the ephod, the breastpiece and the turban. The significance of these clothes is conveyed most clearly by the turban which had a gold plate set on it, inscribed with the words, 'Holy to the Lord'. It is no good being involved in intercession unless we are clothed in the righteousness of Christ and involved in holy living. How can we pray on behalf of others if our own lives are not right, or if we are opposing God by our attitudes?

The ephod had two onyx stones placed upon the shoulders. On each stone was engraved the names of six tribes. This was a reminder that the priest had to bear up before God the tribes of his nation. How much do we, as a royal priesthood, bear upon our shoulders the responsibility of praying for our nation?

The breastpiece was often called the breastpiece of judgement. Again the twelve tribes were commemorated by twelve precious stones attached to it, each having the name of one tribe. The nation was to be carried upon the heart, as well as upon the shoulders; not as a detached religious duty but one bound up by deep feelings for that nation. The breastpiece of judgement is a reminder that the priest's duty is to discern what is right and wrong for the nation.-

While such judgement does require a measure of maturity it is the Spirit of God who warns us of dangers for ourselves and others.

Thirdly, the priest was anointed with oil as part of his consecration. Oil, in Scripture, is a symbol of the Holy Spirit. The work of the Spirit is essential in our lives. If we do not have the Spirit of Christ, Paul tells us, then we do not belong to Christ. The New Testament talks about the Holy Spirit being poured out on the believers, and John reminds them of the anointing that they had received from Christ (1 John 2:27). Just as the work of the Holy Spirit is essential to our new birth, our empowering and our sanctification, it is His work that is so important in this whole area of priestly prayer.

One of the clearest statements concerning the assistance that the Holy Spirit gives in prayer is found in Romans 8:26. Paul states there that we do not know how to pray as we ought but the Holy Spirit comes to our aid. Frequently we find ourselves in a dilemma as we pray. Take a person who is seriously ill; do we pray for their recovery or that God will take them into His presence? Do we pray that a strike will come swiftly to an end, or is God doing something in the ensuing chaos? Do we pray that God will remove certain difficulties from us, or pray that God will help us overcome the problems we face?

The Apostle encourages us by saying, 'The Spirit helps our weakness; for we do not know how to pray as we should, but the Spirit Himself intercedes for us with groanings too deep for words . . .' What does it mean when Scripture talks about the Spirit interceding for us 'with groanings that cannot be uttered' (AV)? Fortunately we have a key to understanding this phrase in the same chapter. Paul talks, in verses 22 and 23 of Romans 8, about creation, and refers to all of creation including human kind groaning to be delivered from the decay that we see all around us and wait to receive 'the redemption of our body.' In other words there is a great longing to be free from the futility of the world as it is, and to be changed at the coming of Christ. Therefore when Scripture talks about the Holy

Spirit 'groaning', it simply means that the Spirit of God expresses His deep longings within us. They are not expressed in words at that point, but we begin to sense His feelings. The problem arises in trying to differentiate between our feelings and those of the Spirit. It is only as we pray and express our thoughts, seeking to know His will that we begin to find that there are longings the Spirit of God is implanting within us.

The Apostle continues by pointing out that the Holy Spirit knows the hearts of people, and also knows the mind of God, so consequently is able to pray according to the will of God. That is a tremendous help to us as we pray. We don't really know the hearts of other people as to whether they are sincere or not, or even holding on to sin in their hearts, but the Holy Spirit knows. We don't really know the purposes of God, and how this all fits together, but the Spirit of God does, so He can pray through us according to God's purposes, if we are careful to sense His longings.

There are many times when I have begun by praying, 'Lord I don't know really how to pray about this matter; grant to me the aid of your Holy Spirit.' That doesn't mean that I have then immediately prayed straight down the line of God's will, but as I have begun to pray around the subject, I have felt that God has shown me how to pray.

Scripture also talks about 'praying in the Spirit.' Obviously this is in contrast to praying in the flesh, where our own sinful attitudes dominate our praying. We can pray out of selfishness, bitterness, or revenge. Jealousy may motivate our prayers, or a concern for our own reputation. Often pride predetermines the way we pray in either seeking to justify ourselves, as the Pharisee did in the temple, or we are concerned only with building up our own position. To pray in the Spirit, on the other hand, is to pray according to the will of God, and not simply seek our own interests.

One aspect of 'praying *in* the Spirit' is to pray '*with* the Spirit'; in other words to pray in tongues (1 Corinthians 14:15). Paul contrasts this to praying with the mind. When

23

we pray in tongues, the mind is bypassed because we do not understand the language. There are times when that can be helpful. We are so quick in working everything out in the way we see it, but God has a completely different perspective on matters. When praying in tongues, we pray along with the Spirit, and begin to sense in our spirits something of His purpose. While this is sufficient in itself to bring about a breakthrough in prayer with the right results, there are other times when our minds need enlightening for us to take the matter further, or just for our own understanding. When we pray in tongues, however, we have, at least, prayed in a way that is free from our own prejudices and carnal reactions.

A further element in 'praying in the Spirit' is the link with God's power. I believe that to pray in the Holy Spirit is to pray in the power of the Spirit. The Holy Spirit is the powerful member of the Trinity who moved across the surface of the waters at creation. He is the same Spirit that gave power to the disciples at Pentecost. When we pray according to the Spirit's direction, we have a sense of God's power being at work. Perhaps this is best conveyed by those tremendous words in Ephesians 3:20: 'Now to Him who is able to do exceeding abundantly beyond all we ask or think, according to the power that works within us . . .'

Another area that is vital, when it comes to the work of the Holy Spirit in prayer, is the gift of the discernment of spirits. There are times when, as we consider a matter, the Holy Spirit shows us that there is an evil spirit involved in the situation. Without the revelation of the Holy Spirit, we can come to wrong conclusions based on our faulty human judgement. We may be praying that God will bless a person in his ministry when he is actually motivated by a deceiving spirit and he is, in fact, a false prophet.

The Holy Spirit is able to give revelation in other ways. It may come in the form of a vision, a dream, or the reminder of a scripture which has a bearing on the specific issue being covered by prayer. Some years ago at an Intercessors For Britain Day of Prayer, God gave a vision and a word of prophecy when we were praying for Northern

Ireland. God showed in the vision a corridor reaching across from Ulster with the powers of darkness trying to move across to England. The prophecy warned us that Satan was seeking to open up a way from Northern Ireland to bring terror on the mainland, and if we were not vigilant in prayer, blood would flow in the streets of mainland Britain. Shortly afterwards an IRA bomb exploded in London. We believe that God was warning us of the dangers, and that He saved us from greater carnage.

When the priest was anointed with oil, something very important was being symbolised: As a royal priesthood we cannot possibly carry on our ministry without the anointing of the Spirit.

The Levitical ceremony of anointing with oil was followed by the offering of three sacrifices. The first was the sin offering. Our priestly function can only continue as we allow Jesus, our sin-bearer, to deal with our sin. Sin becomes a barrier between us and God, but, thank God, Jesus was offered as a sacrifice for sin once and for all.

Then followed the burnt offering. The Old Testament sacrifices point to the Lord Jesus Christ, and yet there is an application for us. The burnt offering was completely offered to God and all that remained at the end was ash. Jesus offered Himself so completely to the Father that He emptied Himself and made Himself of no reputation. When Aaron and his sons offered up their burnt offering, they were likewise implying that they were totally offered up for God and that all their desires, ambitions and their reputations were placed on the altar to be consumed. If we are to be engaged in the priestly ministry of prayer, we also need to lay down our aspirations and ambitions. When we claim in our songs to be a royal priesthood, we are saying that we are totally available, as priests, to serve the King of Kings.

Finally, the ram of ordination was offered to God. Some of the blood from the animal was placed on the right ear, the right thumb and right toe of the priest. In his ministry, the blood had to be applied, literally, from head to toe.

The right side was significant in that it represented a man's strength. In a similar way when we are involved in the priestly ministry every part needs to be cleansed by the blood of Christ and especially our human strength. We so often think that our strengths are all right, and our weaknesses are the problem. Moses first tried to solve his people's problems in his own strength and ended up committing murder. Our strengths need covering as much as our weaknesses because with God it is not by might nor by power but by His Spirit that He will achieve things through us.

As part of the ram was offered up to God, some unleavened bread and one unleavened cake was also offered up. Leaven represents sin, and the very fact that it is unleavened bread and cake is a reminder that we cannot present what is sinful to God. The priest must be without sin. Of course, we do commit sin from time to time, but it must be recognised immediately and confessed. The psalmist asks the question, 'Who may ascend into the hill of the Lord?' His answer is 'He who has clean hands and a pure heart, who has not lifted up his soul to falsehood, and has not sworn deceitfully' (Psalm 24:4). It is for this reason that Paul states that we should pray 'lifting up holy hands, without wrath and dissension' (1 Timothy 2:8). As we come to God in prayer we need to make sure that we are free from sin or wrong reactions.

Again some oil and some of the blood of the ordination ram was sprinkled on the priest and his clothes. Everything needs cleansing with blood, and to be touched by the Holy Spirit. I believe that some of our worship is very fleshly. We start to enjoy ourselves rather than to bring pure worship to God. Having begun in the Spirit, we can end up in the flesh. Our praying can be just as carnal, so everything needs cleansing by the blood and sanctifying by the Spirit.

Part of the ram of ordination was offered to God, but part of it was eaten by the priest. It was almost as if the ordination to the priestly ministry had to become part of him. It had to get inside of him. Our sense of calling to the royal priesthood has to become part of us, realising that we belong to God.

The last point to note is that the ordination ceremony lasted seven days. It is not just for Sunday or any other one day, but for every day of the week. As a royal priesthood we are in the service of the King and are consecrated to Him for every day. There are no days off in His service although there may be days when we can relax. We need, however, to come into His presence daily.

Some shrink back from the task of intercession, but the very fact that we enter into this ministry along with Jesus, the Great Intercessor, ought to encourage us as royal priests. I believe God wants individuals and churches to be functioning much more as a royal priesthood. The early church majored on four things: the apostles' doctrine (teaching), fellowship, breaking bread, and prayer (Acts 2:42). It is probably prayer that is neglected more than anything else in the Church today. When the Church rediscovers its function of intercession, then we shall see a land which is brought back to God. The call that Joel issued to the priests is surely one that is relevant to us. 'Let the priests, the Lord's ministers, weep between the porch and the altar, and let them say, "Spare Thy people, O Lord, and do not make Thine inheritance a reproach, a byword among the nations" ' (Joel 2:17).

4

Standing in the Gap

One of the most amazing of all Scriptures concerning intercession is found in Ezekiel 22:30. God says, 'I searched for a man among them who should build up the wall and stand in the gap before Me for the Land, that I should not destroy it; but I found no one. Thus I have poured out my indignation on them; I have consumed them with the fire of my wrath; their way I have brought upon their own heads.'

In this chapter of Ezekiel, God complains that the prophets have brought false visions and lies; the priests have not taught the difference between right and wrong living, while the princes had corruptly destroyed lives to obtain further wealth. As for the people, they had practised oppression and robbery, and cheated the poor; yet God was looking for just one man who would stand in the gap before Him so that He could turn away from His fierce anger.

I am amazed that even when God sees that a situation is ripe for judgement, He is willing to turn away from His anger. It is as if God has a way to change a situation if one man will intercede for a nation. He becomes a channel through which God can begin to pour His blessing. It seems also that God is pleased when a nation's sin is recognised and acknowledged. Again and again God has had His man to stand in the gap.

The clearest evidence we have is in the case of Moses. It says in Psalm 106:23 'God said that He would destroy them (Israel), had not Moses His chosen one stood in the breach before Him, to turn away His wrath from destroying them.'

At the time when Aaron had created the golden calf and the nation had turned to idolatry and immorality, God threatened to destroy the Israelites and begin afresh with Moses. Moses then begins to argue the case with God, reminding Him that He had brought them out of Egypt. If He destroyed them now, the Egyptians would say that God wasn't capable of bringing them into the Promised Land. He reminds God of the promise made to Abraham, Isaac and Jacob that the people would be numerous and they would enter the land God was giving them. As a result of Moses' petition on behalf of Israel, God turns away from His anger. Just a chapter later (Exodus 33), Moses, as he prays to God concerning the people, receives that delightful promise from the Lord when He says, 'My presence shall go with you, and I will give you rest.' From the complete account we can see that God did, in a measure, punish the Israelites, but through Moses' intercession God had turned from His fierce anger and even promised that His presence would be with them.

There is another occasion, when, at Kadesh Barnea, the people deliberately disobeyed God and failed to enter the Promised Land. Again Moses pleaded with God not to destroy the nation. The basis of his plea is their deliverance from Egypt; God's promise to Abraham, Isaac and Jacob; but also the Egyptians would say He had brought them out of the land to slay them in the wilderness. His final appeal is to remind God that Israel is His inheritance. Consequently the nation is once again spared, but judgement comes upon them in the form of forty years wandering in the wilderness. On both occasions, however, a real measure of God's anger is turned away because Moses stood in the gap before God.

Unfortunately, within Britain today we have to stand in the gap frequently to ask God to remember mercy in time of judgement. Some of us have been aware of God's judgement upon the nation. On at least three occasions, within IFB meetings, there have been visions of God's hands no longer around Britain in protection. On one occasion God was seen allowing foul spirits to invade our shores.

There was a point, in the late Summer of 1984, when Britain was poised on the edge of disaster. We were holding a Prayer and Bible Week in Swanwick at the time. The dockers were threatening to come out on strike in support of the miners. We had already seen some of the worst confrontation between police and pickets that Britain had ever witnessed in an industrial dispute. If the dockers joined the strike, Britain would be paralysed and would be in the hands of strike committees, and the government would be in danger of being brought down. For forty-eight hours the situation swung first one way and then the other. Some docks first decided against strike action and then, for, as pressure was exerted upon them. We could only plead with God on the grounds of His mercy. Then in that Prayer and Bible Week came the break-through. We felt that we could say to the principalities and powers behind the strikes, 'Thus far and no further!' From the next morning onwards support from the dockers began to wane and many stated clearly that they wished to have nothing to do with a political strike, for that is how they saw the strike. I personally believe that all through that year-long strike there was an impression of God's judgement upon our nation.

One thing is very clear in Scripture, and that is, we need to recognise the sin of a nation. We have a record in Daniel 9 of how this prophet-cum-intercessor had noticed how Jeremiah had prophesied that Jerusalem would suffer for 70 years. As a result, he gave himself to prayer, fasting and seeking God. During this time he confesses the sin of the nation and admits that the nation has fallen justifiably under God's judgement. Only after spending considerable time in confessing the nation's sin does he turn his attention to asking that God will restore His glory to Jerusalem and turn His wrath away from the city. Nehemiah in a similar way confessed the sin of Judah before praying that God would raise up the walls of Jerusalem.

Frequently, we have found it necessary, when praying for our nation, to confess, first of all, the sin of our country. Yet, most of all, we have had to turn our attention to the Church. In 1976, during the drought, God began to show at a Prayer and Bible Week, that He was displeased with the Church. The nation had sinned but the Church had failed, in so many ways, to be a holy people. Only when the sin of the Church had been confessed, was there any real liberty to pray for rain. At the end of the Prayer and Bible Week, rain was falling all over Britain. If we as Christians do not act as light and salt, then society becomes corrupt. Perhaps in this, more than anything else, the Church has failed. As in Ezekiel's time, our ministers have not differentiated between the clean and the unclean; for instance, there are churches for practising homosexuals. God's word is very clear about the practice of homosexuality; it is an abomination in His sight. In recent years we have had to listen to church leaders questioning the virgin birth and the bodily resurrection of Jesus. One theologian recently referred to Jesus' death as being merely a brave act of sacrifice, and Jesus as being 'a failed apocalyptic prophet.' The divinity of Jesus has been denied by a variety of theologians. No wonder God has frequently brought us back to the place where we have to confess the sin of the Church.

In 2 Chronicles 7:14 we find God's answer to Solomon's prayer when the temple was dedicated. God says, 'If my people who are called by My name humble themselves and pray, and seek My face and turn from their wicked ways, then I will hear from heaven, will forgive their sin, and will heal their land.' Although this was first spoken to Israel, we shall see later that God still deals with nations on this basis. It is therefore important that we who bear the Lord's name, as His people, need to make sure we fulfil the conditions laid down in this promise.

The first requirement is that we should humble ourselves. We tend to be proud of our churches, proud of our spiritual standing, but not humble enough to come before God and cry out for His help, especially for our nation.

Secondly, we are called to pray. We have so many activities in our church life, but we make little room for strong

31

prayer and intercession. The prayer meeting is the most neglected of all our meetings.

Thirdly, God wants us to seek His face. So often we are too busy to seek a personal encounter with Him. The face is particularly important because it expresses so much. When we look into the face of God, we begin to appreciate His feelings. We can be so busy talking to Him that we do not really recognise His reactions. Churches are accustomed to making plans and then asking God to bless them, instead of waiting upon God for Him to reveal His thoughts. Seeking His face means that we are intent on having a real relationship with the Head of the Church and taking time to listen.

Finally, God asks us to turn from our wicked ways. That includes individual Christians, and also churches. Why does adultery go unchecked in our churches? Ministers guilty of wrong relationships are often moved, rather than removed from office. Spiritualists are allowed to participate in church life, and many churches are riddled with Freemasonry. Those who deny the essentials of the gospel, such as the resurrection or the divinity of Christ, are allowed to go on preaching. The early church would have seen them as false prophets or enemies of the gospel. God requires a holy people. When we fulfil these conditions of humbling ourselves, praying, seeking His face, and turning from our wicked ways, then God will hear, will forgive and heal our land.

God is still waiting for us to stand in the breach. He is still looking for the right people to intercede for the nation. The tragedy is that so often we have to come confessing the sins of the Church before we can make a start on the nation. We need to pray that God will refine His Church and remove that which is unholy. It is interesting that sometimes the media seems to recognise the hand of God more readily than the Church. When York Minster was struck by lightning, it was the secular press who suggested it was an act of God's judgement in response to the consecration of a bishop who had denied the bodily resurrection of Christ!

I recognise that much of what I have written about the Church could be considered unbalanced. I have written generally of the Church and concentrated on its areas of failure. However, there is much to encourage and rejoice about as God has been renewing His Church. God's purposes for His Church, as revealed in Scripture, are absolutely amazing. Let's make sure that we press on into all that God has for His people and expects from them. Many of us feel that while we are under a measure of God's judgement, He is still remembering mercy. I think that is, in no small measure, due to so many who are committed to pray for their nation. I am not thinking of those within Intercessors For Britain only, but many other similar organisations, and some without any organisation who are praying for our Land. They have learnt to stand in the gap, and, as a result, we are experiencing a measure of mercy. May it increase, as our intercessions increase.

5

Praying for Governments

One of the clearest directions given to Christians concerning prayer is found in 1 Timothy 2:1ff. After a general encouragement to pray for all men, Paul specifically narrows down the field to pray for all those in authority, including kings. He is quite clear why this is necessary; so that we may have a tranquil and quiet life marked by godliness and dignity. That is then linked with the fact that Jesus came as a mediator between man and God, and that God desires all men to be saved and to come to a knowledge of the truth.

There is obviously a clear link between good government and men and women being saved. In the first place, we are to pray that those who are in authority will so govern that we may have peace. War may make it much more difficult for the gospel to be proclaimed – especially for missionaries to gain entrance in countries suffering enemy attack.

During the Second World War, there were those who prayed that the Bible Lands would remain open to the gospel. Many prayed, particularly, that Palestine would remain free for the gospel's sake. They prayed also that Palestine would remain free for the sake of many Jews who had taken refuge there from the holocaust in Germany. Rees Howells said at that time, 'Unless God will intervene on behalf of Palestine, there will be no safety there for the Jews. These Bible Lands must be protected, because it is to these lands the Saviour will come back. If I had the choice today (4th July, 1942) I would say to God, "Take all I have but preserve Palestine." We want to say that unless there is a special reason for Egypt to fall, don't let

Alexandria be taken, but give Rommel a setback.'[1] It was that very weekend that the tide turned at El Alamein and Rommel's crack Africa Korps suffered its first major setback.

The second factor about good government is that we need to pray for godliness and dignity. In other words there is a respect for God and a respect for people. I believe that both are essential for the gospel. One of the important parts of the gospel message is God's love for all mankind, no matter what their race, or class; Jesus has died for all, therefore all are important. A society that debases mankind makes it difficult for people to know and feel that there is a God who loves them. That is the problem with apartheid; it causes many black people to look for an answer in Marxism and revolution rather than spiritual answers.

A more important factor, perhaps, is reverence for God. If we have a government that has no respect for God, the proclamation of the gospel becomes more difficult. An evangelist, who for many years had preached the gospel in Mozambique, commented to a leading intercessor that he could not understand why some people spent so much time praying for governments. A few years later, when the door for the gospel into Mozambique had closed, the evangelist commented to the intercessor, 'I now understand why you pray so much for governments, and national and international situations.'

In Britain today, we face a situation where the spread of occultism leaves many in bondage to Satan. Their eyes are blinded to the truth, and there is an atmosphere created that makes a response to the gospel much more difficult. The whole spiritual climate is affected by people having no respect for God. It is a clear violation of God's command not to be involved in spiritism, Satan worship, witchcraft and fortune-telling (see Deuteronomy 18:10–14), yet everywhere these things are mushrooming. Book shops are littered with such trash. New Age Festivals linked with yoga, transcendental meditation, spiritism (spiritualism), and many other aspects of the occult are being held in

[1]*Rees Howells Intercessor*, Ben Grubb, p. 266.

many of our major cities. These things not only bring the judgement of God upon our nation but they strengthen the grip of Satan upon our land.

We cannot legislate against these matters very easily, but successive governments have liberalised our laws, removed censorship, and undermined Christian values of marriage and family life in making divorce easier. It all helps to create a climate of opinion that says, in effect, 'God's laws are not important.' Legislation which would have allowed Sunday trading would have signalled that materialism is more important than spiritual values. Basically, it is a rejection of God which, in the end, causes a society to become increasingly anti-God and therefore more difficult to save.

There are elements at work in our society that have a damaging effect upon our nation. The gay rights movement again creates an atmosphere that makes the acceptance of the good news that much harder. A blasphemous poem portraying Jesus as having a homosexual relationship, was published in *Gay News* some time ago. (Mary Whitehouse brought a successful prosecution for blasphemy against the publication.) The poem revealed an attitude towards Christ, that is seen in society, which debases His nature and undermines the essential elements in salvation; namely, His divinity and perfection. It seems that there is an area here where a spirit of perversity is seeking to distort and destroy. When we reject the truth of God, we lay ourselves open to every deceiving and foul spirit.

Paul, in Romans 1, shows that there is a descending scale of depravity. When we reject the truth about God, we become open to futile speculations which darken the minds of men. The Apostle makes it clear that there comes a point at which God progressively gives man over to impurity, degrading passions (lesbianism and homosexuality) and finally a depraved mind. Laws which permitted homosexual practices between consenting adults have helped to debase our society.

Being aware of how the gay rights movement could help to produce a society that was even more reminiscent of Sodom and Gomorrah, we felt it was essential, during the election of 1979, to pray for righteous people to be elected to Parliament. There was already one MP who was a practising lesbian, and many others were pressing for reforms on gay rights issues. We felt, within IFB, that it was necessary to pray that God would remove from Parliament the campaigners for gay rights. It was with a great sense of relief that we found that the lesbian MP failed to get re-elected together with several others who supported this cause.

Unfortunately, we have forgotten to pray for all those in authority. Since 1979, what Satan failed to do through national government, he has sought to do through local politics. Many London boroughs have policies of positive discrimination giving preference to homosexuals and lesbians in areas of social work, including the care of children. Councillors have encouraged gay groups with all sorts of grants and help. The scouts had money withheld from them, by way of grants, unless they were prepared to allow homosexuals into their organisation. This was later reversed, but it shows all too clearly the battle that is being waged in our land. There is a spirit of perversity very much at work in our national capital, and we Christians have failed to protest and pray as we ought. As a result of these policies, we, as a nation, are coming under the judgement of God because of these trends.

We need to continue to pray over our local councils. Some councils have placed governors in Church Schools as a way of trying to gain greater control of these schools even to the extent of trying to appoint non-Christians into those schools as Head Teachers. This has been attempted, although it is against the rules of the diocesan education authorities for non-Christians to be appointed as Head Teachers. We need to be aware of these battles as Christians, and pray for those in authority in local councils.

Some years ago Jens Thorsen wanted to make a blasphemous film about the life of Christ. He was even going to receive a grant of money from the Danish Government to assist with this film. Christians within Intercessors for Denmark felt so incensed about this matter that they called upon God to intervene. After several days of seeking God, they felt that He was leading them to pray for four things. First of all, they prayed that God would stir the Pope to action. Secondly, they prayed that France would withdraw permission for Thorsen to film in that country. Thirdly, they prayed that the Danish Government would withdraw the financial assistance for the film. Finally, they felt that God would bring down the Danish Government for its support of the film.

Within a week the Pope had spoken out against the film. This then caused France to withdraw permission for filming, and ordered Thorsen to leave the country. Two months later the Danish Government grew so concerned about its own position that it withdrew the grant. Just two weeks after that, the government fell, and a new coalition government came to power. This was headed by a Christian who had a clear Christian witness and upheld the law of blasphemy which the previous government had tried to abolish. Consequently, this diabolical film was never made in spite of various attempts in other countries. Governments can affect so much the very ethos of a country for good or ill, and, in the long run, for the entrance of, or the opposition to, the gospel.

There are other areas of authority for which we must pray including the police, magistrates and even employers and unions. A couple of years ago there was a frightful confrontation between Mr. Eddie Shah of the Messenger Newspaper and the NGA (National Graphical Association). We felt as a Church that the scenes of violence and intimidation had gone beyond the bounds of peaceful protest and picketing. As we prayed, we felt that a spirit of lawlessness was involved which sought to create such violence and brutality. We therefore felt it right to pray for an end to the riotous behaviour. There came the point where we felt that God gave us authority to bind the evil spirit, and there was an immediate return to peace on the picket line. In this particular case, it came about by the NGA being taken to court for the scenes which took place on the picket lines and for being in contempt of court for its action. We have seen at other times, such as during the miners' strike, that as God has given us authority to bind the spirit of lawlessness, there has been a return to peaceful picketing.

In this matter of a lawless spirit, we have been aware that the same spirit has operated in many inner city riots. Again, we have found that as we have prayed God has given us authority to bind the spirit, and calm has returned to our cities. I remember very well a situation during the Toxteth riots in 1981. I had been at a meeting in Lytham St. Annes and returned to find that people were expecting trouble in Moreton that night; some shopkeepers had boarded up their windows. I contacted the House Group leaders of our fellowship, and within the hour, we had a prayer meeting taking place in our home. We prayed for Moreton and the neighbouring estates on the Wirral which had been affected by copy-cat riots similar to those in Toxteth. We prayed especially for Toxteth that the riots would come to an end. There had already been rioting over a number of nights, and we were concerned about the general level of violence in the area. Having prayed about the whole area for nearly two hours, we felt that God gave us that clear note of authority to bind the spirit of lawlessness over the whole Merseyside area and especially Toxteth. We firmly believed that the level of violence would now decrease. As we drew the meeting to a close, I remember asking God, that as youths came out of the pubs they would not congregate in groups and cause trouble. I asked God to scatter them with His 'water-cannon' from the heavens if necessary. The other thing I asked God was that now the lawless spirit had been bound, would He release His Holy Spirit to save people? I suddenly remembered the husband of one of our members who was there in the meeting, and prayed, 'Lord, will you save Arthur.' Then we went to our homes.

It wasn't long before I began to receive news of answered prayer. There was no trouble in Moreton that night. Two of our members were on duty as special constables when a group of youths began to gather together. As they did so, it began to rain and the group quickly dispersed, much to the relief of the two men on duty! Just four hours after our prayer-meeting, Arthur was watching television, when suddenly the set went off for no explicable reason. As he sat staring at the blackened screen, he felt that God was speaking to Him. He knew the way of salvation from his teens but had never surrendered his life to Christ. There and then God met him and saved him as Arthur recalled the gospel. We also learnt that the rioting in Toxteth had been on a smaller scale that night and each night became progressively quieter. That had proved to be a most remarkable night, but only because we had made a break-through in prayer, and had God's permission to bind the spirit of lawlessness.

While I may have touched here on matters related specifically to spiritual warfare that will concern us in a later chapter, nevertheless, I have endeavoured to point out that we need to pray for all those in authority that we may lead a tranquil and godly existence as a nation. That will include the police, magistrates, employers, unions, governments and councils. All of these create something of the right climate for the gospel. Where laws and attitudes allow a liberalisation and rebellion against God, then it becomes more difficult to preach the gospel. Lawlessness and rebellion in civil matters is, basically, an expression of lawlessness against God. We may need to pray against the demonic forces that would rob us of our peace and godly living but most of all we need to pray that those in authority will help create a climate that assists the gospel, instead of hindering it.

6

The Falklands War

We have already seen the importance of praying for governments in relationship to the gospel, but it is equally clear in Scripture that nations are judged by God on the basis of their moral integrity. When Jeremiah went down to the potter's house, God showed him that He was more than capable of destroying and remaking. Then came the prophetic word: 'At one moment I might speak concerning a nation or concerning a kingdom to uproot, to pull down, or to destroy it, if that nation against which I have spoken turns from its evil, I will relent concerning the calamity I planned to bring on it.' (Jeremiah 18:7,8) God goes on to say that the reverse is true; if a nation is under God's blessing and then sins, He will bring evil against it.

The Book of Amos begins with a series of messages against various nations for their sin, and through almost every other Old Testament prophet, God speaks of His judgement against the nations, or promises His blessing on others. In Paul's address at Athens, he states: 'God made from one, every nation of mankind to live on all the face of the earth, having determined their appointed times, and the boundaries of their habitation, that they should seek God, if perhaps they might grope for Him and find Him, though He is not far from each one of us' (Acts 17:26,27). God obviously deals with the borders of the nations and fixes how long those nations and borders shall last. Paul also makes it clear that those boundaries are fixed so that people might seek God and find Him. An obvious example of that is South Korea. Many Christians in Korea believe that God held back the Communist forces at the 38th parallel in response to prayer. Certainly there is a different spiritual atmosphere between North and South Korea. In the north there is an oppressive government that seeks to destroy the Church, but in the south, there is a mighty move of God's Spirit so that 25% are born-again Christians. If the present rate of growth continues, it has been estimated that by the end of the century 50% of the population will be Christian. If ever a boundary was vital for people to seek after God and find him, then that border is.

Scripture also states very clearly that God raises up rulers and removes them. It was inevitable that Hitler should eventually be defeated because of the wickedness of the Nazi regime. Similarly some of us prayed that God would either change Idi Amin or remove him. The day came when his reign of terror came to an end.

It is difficult for some Christians to accept that God actually brings about wars. Habakkuk had a problem in this respect. He had been praying for his country and asking God to do something about the violence in the land. God's reply was: 'I am doing something in your days – you would not believe it if you were told.' The gist of the message, which was so difficult to accept, was that God was going to bring the Chaldeans, a fierce and cruel people, against Israel. After great difficulty Habakkuk got the message and realised that even if everything was destroyed he would still exult in the Lord, and rejoice in the God of his salvation.

Two days before the Falkland Islands were invaded by Argentine forces, one of our members who is a Kelper (a native of the islands) heard a crash in her living room and discovered that her plaque of the Falklands had fallen from her wall. She felt, in that moment, that God had shown her that in the heavenlies, the place where battles are really fought, the Falkland Islands had already fallen. Unknown to us at the time, there was an emergency session of the cabinet on that same day, Wednesday, 31st March, 1982. All next day, President Reagan attempted to phone the President of Argentina. Finally, in the evening, he managed to contact him, but failed to prevent the invasion of the Islands. By 8.30 the following morning the fighting for the Islands was over and a cease fire had been announced with the Argentinians fully in control.

It was some time later that the news broke in Britain. We were stunned and horrified. It was almost with unbelief that many of us listened to the news reports, and heard the emergency debate in the House of Commons on the Saturday morning. I remember doing some gardening, listening to every word of the debate on the radio. Mrs Thatcher announced to a packed and subdued house that a large task force would be assembled and set sail for the south Atlantic as soon as possible.

It is our practice as a fellowship to have three weeks of prayer a year. This does not rule out other occasions, but we always have a week of prayer at the New Year, Easter and September. It so happened, therefore, that just three days after the invasion of the Falklands, we commenced a week of prayer. We spent five evenings (Monday to Good Friday) spreading the whole matter of the invasion before the Lord. That week was followed by two weeks of early morning prayer meetings at 6.30 to pray through every aspect of the issue. Later we felt challenged that having prayed about the conflict, and having sacrificed our sleep over some remote islands in the south Atlantic, we ought to have another week when we rose early to pray for men and women in Britain to be saved. We can be so stirred about temporal matters, but neglect weightier eternal issues.

I cannot now distinguish exactly the order in which we prayed about the various items, but I do remember very clearly how God led us. During the first week's prayer, we felt that God showed us that war would come. Various attempts were being made for peace talks and to find solutions through the United Nations Organisation. Increasingly we were sure that there would be a conflict. The main reason for our conviction was that it seemed a time of judgement had come for the Galtieri Government with its appalling policy on human rights. We felt that God

43

wanted to remove the leaders, and that only by Argentina being defeated would this come about. Even now, I find it staggering to recall how clearly we saw this outcome. Later of course, this is exactly what happened and the military dictatorship of General Galtieri came to an end.

One night during that first week of prayer, the young lady who had come from the Falklands a few years before, and was now a member of our fellowship, had a dream – or was it a vision? She wasn't sure. Suddenly she was woken up sensing that a black horse was trying to break in at the back door. It was being pursued by a pale coloured horse. Then they disappeared out of view, but she knew that they were fighting. Eventually the pale horse came back limping but victorious. It seemed to us, at that time that God was saying that although the Argentine forces had broken into the Falklands, they would be pursued by the Task Force which would ultimately be victorious, but at a cost. It is always difficult in retrospect to know just how much we fully appreciated what God was saying, but this at least was something of the impression that we had as a result of the vision.

At the end of that first week of prayer, we held an early morning communion service on Easter Sunday. At the end, we prayed especially for this Falkland Island girl and her family. God spoke to her in prophecy commencing with the words: 'Fear not the bloodshed that is to come . . .' I remember recalling these words several times over the next couple of weeks. I do not recall the rest of the words of that prophecy, but God was reassuring her that she need not fear for her brother and sisters still in the Falklands. God did, in fact, keep every one of them safe. It seemed very clear, however, at the end of that first week, from all that we were sensing in prayer, vision and prophecy that there was war ahead.

In those early days we sensed that Lord Carrington could be removed as Foreign Secretary. For some time we had prayed about him concerning his dealings with Israel. It seemed that he was far more supportive of the Arab countries than Israel. We as a Church had become convinced that God had restored that nation. Jesus said that Jerusalem would 'be trampled under foot by the gentiles until the times of the gentiles be fulfilled' (Luke 21:24). For the first time since Christ, Jerusalem was again in Jewish hands following the 1967 war. Jesus had also been asked by His disciples, 'Lord, is it at this time You are restoring the Kingdom to Israel?' Jesus replied, 'It is not for you to know times or epochs which the Father has fixed by His own authority' (Acts 1:6,7). If the sovereignty of Israel was not to be restored Jesus would clearly have said so rather than allow His disciples to be under a misapprehension. His reply suggests that it would happen, but the timing was not their concern.

In the Old Testament the promise was given to Abraham that the Land of Canaan was to be given to him and his descendants as an *Everlasting Possession*. God makes it plain that Ishmael is not included in that promise but Isaac who was yet to be born. Esau is also excluded from the promise as Mt Seir is given to him and his descendants. The promise is later confirmed to Jacob (Israel) and his descendants, again as an everlasting possession (see Genesis 17:7,8,18–20; 48:4). There are also many other references in the prophets to a restoration other than that following the Babylonian exile.

Lord Carrington was on a Middle East tour when the Falklands War broke out. He had been supporting the claims of the Arabs for the land, gained during the 1967 Arab-Israeli War, to be returned, which included part of Jerusalem. He had also previously gone to Saudi Arabia following the T.V. showing of 'The Death of a Princess.' It had caused a great offence to the House of Saud, but most observers felt that although it was presented as fiction, it was based on fact. Being aware that Lord Carrington may have failed to read the danger signals of a possible invasion of the Falkland Islands, we prayed that God would remove him from the Foreign Office, replacing him with somebody more sympathetic to Israel's plight who would not be working against the purposes of God. After all, God has said that those who bless Israel, He will bless, and those who curse Israel, He will curse. Soon afterwards Lord Carrington was forced to resign because of the Falkland invasion. It seemed that God was certainly dealing with the leaders of the nations in this whole matter, not only General Galtieri but our own Foreign Office. It is true that God 'reduces the rulers to nothing, and makes the judges of the earth meaningless' (Isaiah 40:23).

As the British Task Force was sailing towards the Southern Atlantic, we prayed that God would save those within the armed forces who would be part of the invasion force or who would be sailing into the danger zone. We felt that many of them would begin to consider, at least in their own minds, life and death issues and what might lay beyond the grave. We discovered later that Bible studies were held on the ships of the Task Force and many came to the Lord as a result. There has also been a flourishing Christian fellowship among members of the armed forces who have been stationed in the Falklands since the British regained power. Again we praise God for answers to prayer.

We were aware, of course, that we could not pray from a prejudiced point of view. God sent Jesus to die for the Argentinians as well as for the British. We prayed that Argentine soldiers would be saved and that God would move upon that country in a mighty way by His Spirit. We knew that God was already at work in that country in bringing thousands to Himself, but again we have heard from missionaries in South America, that those revival fires have increased since the Falkland invasion. We would like to feel that our prayers at that time of national crisis had some part to play, along with other Christians praying for Argentina, in bringing a real move of God's Spirit.

Another aspect that occupied our prayers was the weather. We knew that winter would be closing in fast upon those Islands. Snow and rough seas would hamper the Task Force in making a landing. We prayed that God would send good weather to assist our troops. Harry Bagnall, the Anglican chaplain at the Cathedral in Port Stanley wrote in his book,[1] 'And still the incredible weather

[1]*Faith Under Fire*, p. 107

continued . . . the onset of winter was delayed by day after day of sunshine and winds that were tolerable'

As the Task Force took up its position near the Falklands, we listened for any clues from the news that might help us to know how to pray more effectively. Consequently we tuned into the 6 a.m. news before going to the Prayer Meeting. We realised that some attempt would be made to put men ashore to spy out the land. We prayed that they would be successful in their landing, and eventually establish a beach-head. Again it was encouraging to learn later that a party of men had been put ashore at Pebble Island on the 13th May and a raid was made the next day, destroying the radar station, ammunition and fuel depots, together with eleven enemy aircraft. Just six days later the main force landed at San Carlos Bay and a successful bridge-head had been established.

We realised that lives would be lost on both sides, and this brought a sombre note to our praying. Then came the sinking of the Belgrano, with the loss of many Argentine lives and the horrifying attacks on British ships. I cannot pretend we found answers to all the questions which arose in our minds concerning war, death and protection, but we did feel it right to pray that God would protect those who loved Him. Those who have committed their lives to Christ are under His protection in a way that non-Christians are not. I am not going to say that every born-again Christian was saved from death; after all Jesus died on behalf of others. On the other hand we have to say that there were some amazing stories of survival. I read of one platoon, under the leadership of a Christian, which was able to take a strategic position without a single man being lost. He had prayed for the protection of his men.

I remember hearing Derek Prince say that in the Second World War men were pleased to be with him as an officer because they always felt safe with him. They were somehow aware of God's protection because of this man's faith. I believe that the point Derek was making was a valid one; there is a protection for the people of God, as we walk in obedience. We prayed for the same protection for believers amongst the Argentine forces and that God would use their witness.

We prayed for the Falkland Islanders themselves. Again as we prayed we felt that there was a measure of judgement upon the Kelpers. Their way of life was far removed from the Lord, generally speaking. They were often hard drinkers, and immorality was common. Many were involved in the occult, and most of the Islanders were hardened against the Lord. The Kelper, in our congregation, recalled how, as a teenager, when anyone who was born again came to the Islands they were regarded as some strange breed who were not to be trusted.

We prayed that God would physically protect the Kelpers during the fighting. It was amazing that in all the bombardment which took place over Port Stanley only two people were killed and a third, later, died of injuries. There were no other serious injuries, but many remarkable escapes. We prayed that through all the fighting and danger the Islanders would turn to the Lord. I have to say that this is an area where we saw no break-throughs in response to prayer. There has been no lasting work done among the Kelpers, with scarcely any turning to the Lord as far as we know. While there was an increase in the number attending worship during the invasion and the following weeks, the numbers have since fallen. If the invasion was a measure of God's judgement upon the Islanders, what awaits them in the future if they do not heed the voice of God in their situation?

The only ground of hope is that, perhaps, some of the Christians among the armed forces might be able to share their faith with the Falkland Islanders. Maybe, the Kelpers who do know Christ will begin to lift their voice in prayer for the salvation of their people and for the defeat of the enemy of our souls.

Two people we remembered much in our prayers were Harry and Iris Bagnall who were leading the Anglican work at the Cathedral in Port Stanley. We prayed for their protection and God's blessing upon their work. We know that many servicemen have been thankful for their open home, and for the encouragement that they have brought.

What of the future? God alone knows. I only know that we learnt much in listening and praying during those weeks. Our faith was strengthened in a prayer-answering God. We understood that prayer affects the destiny of nations, and yet, at the same time, it is important to know what God is doing and not just to pursue our own line in prayer. We sense that the final chapter of the Falkland Islands has not yet been written. Is it too late for a people to see the deliverance of God, and find eternal security in Him? Maybe that is a burden that the Falkland Islanders themselves must bring before the throne of grace and find mercy from a gracious God.

7

It's War!

As Christians we seem to treat Satan from one of two extremist viewpoints. Either, we consider that Satan has done a disappearing trick and doesn't really exist, or, we so emphasise his power, that we live in fear of his tactics. Paul, however, was well aware of his strategy because he warned the Corinthian Church to restore to fellowship a brother who had repented, lest he became discouraged and consequently attacked by Satan. Paul then adds the words, 'For we are not ignorant of his schemes' (2 Corinthians 2:11). Unfortunately so often we are.

Probably many Christians can quote freely from Ephesians 6:12 where it says, 'We wrestle not against flesh and blood, but against principalities, against powers . . .' (AV), yet we have not really understood the nature of the battle. The real war is not in terms of people who oppose the gospel, but the spiritual powers behind people. The word 'Satan' means adversary and he most certainly is God's opponent, fighting, every step of the way the purposes of God. To be involved in prayer means that we enter into this spiritual dimension of warfare.

Perhaps the clearest picture of this is seen in Daniel chapter 10. Daniel had spent three weeks fasting and seeking God in order to understand a vision which had been given to him. At the end of the three weeks, an angel appeared stating that from the moment he began to pray, his prayer had been heard. The angel added that as he tried to bring revelation about the vision, he was opposed by the prince of the kingdom of Persia. This battle had gone on for twenty-one days – the entire time that Daniel had been fasting and praying. Only when the Archangel Michael had intervened in the battle was the angel able to bring the message to the prophet. Plainly, the prince of the kingdom of Persia was no ordinary human prince. No human being could restrain an angel in open combat like that. It was a matter of wrestling against the principalities that Paul mentions.

The angel also pointed out to Daniel that the prince of Greece would follow the prince of Persia. Jesus was accused of casting out demons by Beelzebub, the prince of demons. Scripture, therefore, recognises that there are rulers (princes) under Satan's 'kingship' who control certain areas, usually geographical ones. We tend to use the word in that sort of way when we talk about the 'principality of Wales'. A principality, according to the dictionary, is a state ruled by a prince.

In Daniel's case, the prince of the kingdom of Persia was trying to lock everything up. If Daniel came to understand the purposes of God, then he could pray through those plans until they were accomplished, therefore the angel's mission must be stopped at all costs. Satan's strategy was to send the demonic prince, who was responsible for the nation of Persia, to stop the angel. This was such a crucial issue because Cyrus, a Persian King, would later allow the Jews to return to their own land. Obviously, it was essential that they should return, for then the Messiah could come and bring Salvation to the world.

When we take into account these matters we can understand why Daniel had to battle away in prayer and fasting for three whole weeks and why the powers of darkness sought to intervene. We do not fully appreciate the battle that goes on in the heavenlies before certain things can take place on earth.

In Ezekiel 27, we have a lamentation over the town of Tyre. The next chapter is addressed to the ruler of Tyre, but by the time you reach verse 11, you are suddenly brought face to face with the fact that it is no longer an earthly ruler that is being addressed. God says, 'You had the seal of perfection, full of wisdom and perfect in beauty. You were in Eden, the garden of God . . . You were the anointed cherub who covers, and I placed you there. You were on the holy mountain of God . . . You were blameless in your ways from the day you were created, until unrighteousness was found in you.' It was as if behind the city of Tyre, with its wickedness, there was an earthly king who has exalted himself in his arrogance, but was controlled and inspired by Satan himself. The King of Tyre simply becomes a reflection of the usurper, Satan, who fell through pride. As a result, the whole geographical area was now controlled by Satan, through his vassal.

I firmly believe that Satan has put his princes over the nations. Through them he seeks to dominate governments and nations. I believe there is a prince responsible for controlling the British Isles. His mission is to destroy the work of God and bring the nation in subjugation to Satan. That is true of Russia, Iran, and every major nation in the world, and of minor nations as well, to a lesser or greater extent. One of the reasons Scripture talks about the nations coming against Israel, in the last days, is that Satan will seek to motivate those nations to prevent the purposes of God in bringing Israel to Himself, by way of preparation for the return of the Messiah.

In spite of this great global conflict in the heavenly realms, the final victory belongs to Christ. We have a glimpse of this in Revelation 12:7 where the Archangel Michael and his angels make war with Satan and his forces and finally overcome that deceiver and accuser of the brethren. The clear declaration is then made: 'Now the salvation, and the power, and the kingdom of our God and the authority of Christ have come . . .'

In Psalm 2, which is a messianic psalm, we see the Father addressing the Son saying, 'Ask of Me, and I will surely give the nations as Thine inheritance, and the very ends of the earth as Thy possession.' The Book of Revelation confirms this will happen with the words ringing from heaven, 'The Kingdom of the World has become the kingdom of our Lord, and His Christ; and He will reign forever and ever' (Revelation 11:15). We need to understand that, although Satan seeks to exercise his authority over the nations, by his princes, Christ will gain the authority over every nation. We need to rejoice that already Jesus is over every power, authority and name. If we do not live in the light of His victory, realising that He disarmed the powers of darkness on the cross, we will be in danger of depression and despair. We need to remember, though, that there is still a battle to be fought against the principalities and powers, and, like Daniel, we are engaged in the warfare by prayer.

One of the points that is missed more than any other, concerning wrestling against principalities and powers, is that the armour of God is given to us to wage war. When Paul completes his check list of the armour, he piles up the phrases about prayer. He says, 'With all *prayer* and *petition*, *pray* at all times in the Spirit . . . be on the alert with all *perseverence and petition* for all the saints and *pray* on my behalf . . . to make known with boldness the mystery of the gospel . . .' The armour is for our protection, but the real fighting is done in prayer. We need to be watchful for the saints, and to pray against those powers that would oppose the gospel. Most Christians seem to have considered the armour as an end in itself rather than it equipping us for warfare. The vital thing in wrestling against principalities and powers is prayer. That's where the battle is lost or won.

Yongi Cho in his book, *Prayer: Key to Revival*[1] makes it clear as to why the Church in South Korea is seeing thousands won to Christ every month, with miracles and people being delivered. He maintains that there is an open heaven over their country. He continues: 'When a country has an open heaven, there is a freedom and spiritual liberty in preaching the gospel. The level of faith is high and one does not find a great deal of spiritual opposition in a country that has an open heaven. In some countries, it is difficult to preach because there is so much spiritual opposition. Satanic forces that oppose the gospel are strong and there

[1]*Prayer: Key to Revival*, p. 22

53

isn't much faith. . . . Why do we have this spiritual atmosphere? The answer is prayer.'

It took years of constant fighting against the enemy to push back those powers of darkness. We in Britain have hardly started the battle yet, but God is calling us to wage war now. Stop polishing your armour, and be prepared to get it dented in the battle that must be fought!

Paul says, 'The weapons of our warfare are not of the flesh, but divinely powerful for the destruction of fortresses. We are destroying speculations and every lofty thing raised up against the knowledge of God . . .' (2 Corinthians 10:4,5). The religions and philosophies of this world are all speculations that have been raised up against Christ. We cannot come together in some glorious united faith with Hindus, Muslims, Buddhists and Baha'is, as some are advocating, because they are all contrary to the truth that there is 'no other name under heaven whereby men shall be saved' – that name being Jesus Christ. Communism is anti-God; that's its philosophy. All of these beliefs are raised up against Christ. Behind each one of them, and the other world religions and philosophies, there are demonic forces at work seeking to exalt themselves against Christ. That's why the kings of the earth and the rulers 'take counsel together against the Lord and against His Anointed' (Psalm 2:2; Acts 4:26). They are being mobilised by satanic forces to oppose Christ. There is only one thing to do about such demonic speculations: engage in spiritual warfare to destroy such strongholds. We need to note, however, that Paul implies that we can only destroy such satanic strongholds when our 'obedience is complete.'

It is interesting to notice that throughout Israel, and other middle eastern countries, and increasingly in Europe, every mosque with its minaret dominates the surrounding churches and synagogues. A huge mosque is now being built to dominate St. Peter's in Rome. It is as if Paul's words about 'every lofty thing raised up against the knowledge of God' is being expressed literally in the architecture. Islam actually considers itself to be superior to both Judaism and Christianity and to have superseded them both.

A lot of Christians are ignorant of the real nature of Islam. They assume that Muslims worship the same God as ourselves, along with the Jews. Nothing could be further from the truth. 'The Arabs of Mohammed's day worshipped many gods, and the centre of worship was the Kaaba in Mecca (still Islam's most holy place). The Kaaba is a stone structure that orthodox Muslims say has been built or rebuilt ten times. The current Kaaba, built in AD 696, is forty feet by thirty-five feet by fifty feet high. In Mohammed's day 365 gods were worshipped in the Kaaba. Allah was one of these deities and the god of the Quraish tribe, of which Mohammed was a part. For four years after his vision, Mohammed proclaimed more and more openly that Allah was the only god and that he was Allah's prophet.'[2] He had chosen one idol out of all the pantheon of gods at Kaaba.

Muslems believe that ultimately they will dominate the world and destroy all other faiths. Written in the Koran are these words: 'O ye true believers (Muslims) do not become friendly with Jews or Christians! Kill the idol worshippers wherever you find them, take them prisoner, besiege them, lie in wait for them. When you meet unbelievers cut their heads off, make a bloodbath out of it.'[3]

Another statement to be found in the Koran reads: 'Make war upon those who believe not . . . even if they be people of the book (that is Jews and Christians) until they have willingly agreed to pay the Jizya (tax) in recognition of their submissive state.'[4]

It can be seen from these two quotations why the Jews were so often persecuted and badly treated in Muslim countries, and why Christians have suffered badly at their hands as well. In some Arab countries, as soon as somebody confesses to being a Christian, he or she is immediately killed. Many Christians suffered such a fate during the Iranian revolution. We can also understand the whole nature of the jihad (holy war) against the background of

[2]*The Unholy War* Marius Baar p. 58–59
[3]*Ibid* p. 85
[4]*The Dagger of Islam* John Laffin p. 39

such statements from the Koran, and also why it is almost impossible for Arab countries to make peace with Israel. If they do, then they are seen to be traitors to the Arab cause and to the Muslim religion.

We can see, too, how Islam is doctrinally opposed to Christianity in the statement that is found on the frieze of the golden Dome of the Rock (mosque) in Jerusalem. It reads, 'There is no God but Allah! Praise be to Allah who never produced a son, nor had a companion, nor needed a protector. Praise his greatness.'[5] Other similar statements denouncing the trinity are also to be found on the dome. In many ways one feels that already we have on the temple mount the 'abomination of desolation' that Jesus spoke about.

John writes in one of his letters, 'This is the antichrist, the one who denies the Father and the Son. Whoever denies the Son does not have the Father; the one who confesses the Son has the Father also' (1 John 2:22,23). I have no doubt that the spirit of antichrist is at work in Islam and is one of the great deceiving spirits of our time. The great mosque at the Dome of the Rock is venerated by Muslims as the place where Abraham offered up Ishmael. Scripture tells us it was Isaac. In so many ways Islam is based on deception and comes from the Father of lies, Satan, himself.

The avowed aim of Islam is to take Europe, but Muslims believe that if they can win London, then they can conquer the Continent. One Islamic paper printed in Britain urged all Muslims to unite because the west is decadent and, if they stood together, 'the flag of Islam will fly over parliament' and the law would become Islamic. In one London parish a vicar was told by Islamic leaders not to ring the church bells as they considered that part of London to be an Islamic village.

We need to stand against the advancing tide of Islam. We must understand that our battle is not against flesh and blood; we are not fighting Muslims, but, basically, the forces behind the Islamic invasion. We need to pray against the demonic forces behind Islam, so that we may halt,

[5] *The Unholy War* p. 146

not only the advance of this antichrist spirit, but see a breakthrough in bringing these people to Christ. Jesus died for them, but Satan seeks to keep them in bondage by his damnable lies. This is only one of the battles that needs to be fought today in the battle for Britain. We have a tough spiritual warfare ahead of us, if we are to be under an open heaven.

Although Islam may be making great strides forward in many areas, we need to realise that it is not invincible. Recently, in one country on the Continent, some Christians gathered together to pray against a massive new mosque which was under construction. As they prayed factions began to appear within the leadership and the Islamic community. Soon, a complete division took place which hindered the building, and caused financial problems for the construction process. There were also problems of tax being owed to the government, and it now appears that the only way these financial problems are going to be resolved is for the mosque to be auctioned. The Christians are praying that it might eventually become a place of prayer for the nation, as they continue the spiritual battle for their land.

In Paul's description of the various powers of darkness that we wrestle against, Islam would be classed as a 'world ruler'. That is also true of communism. They both seek to dominate the world and reach across international borders. In every country where communism gains control, the Christian Church is persecuted. This has been true in countries from Russia to Cuba, and can be seen in African countries where communism has more recently gained power, such as Ethiopia, Mozambique and Angola. In recent years thousands of churches have been closed in Ethiopia, and hundreds of pastors imprisoned.

Just over a year ago on Merseyside, during the council elections, an extreme left-wing group declared in their publication that when they gain power in Liverpool they will close the churches. The article was illustrated with the photographs of three evangelical churches in the city. The battle is still on in Britain to stifle the gospel of Christ.

Communism, in declaring that there is no God, is also setting itself up as one of those lofty speculations raised up against Christ. Such 'world rulers' will only receive a setback as the Church rises up in prayer. In China today we are seeing, in some places, whole areas won for Christ. Again it is the power of prayer that has made the breakthrough.

Our wrestling is also against a host of evil spirits. We need to be careful in listing these spirits. Some Christians talk about a spirit of laziness or a spirit of greed, but we would do much better to keep to those mentioned in Scripture. Greed and laziness is seen in the Word of God as human failure and sin, not demonic spirits. Those that are mentioned in Scripture are: foul spirit, evil and unclean spirits, as general terms for demonic spirits; deaf and dumb spirits, together with a spirit of infirmity (sickness) which affect health; familiar spirits and a spirit of divination – linked together in spiritism and fortune-telling; a lying spirit, a spirit of antichrist, a perverse spirit, a spirit of error, and a deceiving spirit – leading to deception and often linked with false prophets; a spirit of bondage that brings people into slavery, often to fear, and preventing them from knowing the freedom in Christ, including scriptural truths. There is the mention of a spirit of stupor which could be just a human spirit (attitude), but more likely, demonic activity which prevents people seeing spiritual truths; a spirit of harlotry, and unclean spirits which may be responsible for spiritual as well as physical adultery and immorality; a spirit of fear, and a spirit of heaviness causing fear and oppression, together with a spirit of jealousy which play upon our emotions. Finally, there is a spirit of lawlessness which brings violence, anarchy and antagonism to the law of the land and to God's laws. Satan uses all these spirits as part of his army, under the control of the world rulers and principalities.

It is very easy to become fearful when we consider such a list, but we need to remember that we were delivered from Satan's power when we came to know Christ, and that we are under His protection, when we walk in obedience. When we fall into sin, we need to confess it and come back afresh under the protection of Christ. To do so means that we have on the breastplate of righteousness. If we walk in the truth, we have on the belt of truth and are protected with the helmet of salvation. When we are clad with the armour we can then wage war against the world rulers, the principalities and powers, and the host of demonic forces. If we are rejecting the truth, how can we stand against a spirit of deception? We have already become prone to its attack.

One thing is clear from Scripture; we are involved in a battle. Satan is opposing the purposes of God. There are battles in the heavenlies between Satan's forces and the angels of God. We have the privilege of being involved in the battle by our prayers and intercession. Again and again God waits for our petitions before He moves His battalions into battle. If we fail to watch and pray, then Satan gets the victory, not only in our lives, but in our nation. Isn't it time you stopped polishing your armour and got into the battle? How much more ground does Satan have to take before the Christians stop moaning about the situation and start fighting? It's time for us to go on the offensive and take the land for God.

8

Binding the Strong Man

We have already seen that principalities, powers and world rulers, together with an army of demonic spirits, seek to control individuals, nations, or whole areas of the world, by various religions or philosophies. The Apostle Paul makes an amazing statement in Ephesians 3:10 that God has chosen to reveal 'the administration of the mystery (the gospel) . . . in order that the manifold wisdom of God might now be made known through the church to rulers and the authorities in the heavenly places.'

First of all, the phrase about God's administration comes from the Greek word meaning 'stewardship'. A trusted slave was often left in charge of certain responsibilities which might include the running of his estate. Joseph was such a trusted steward overseeing the affairs of Potipher. God has brought us into His administration, or His government, and given us responsibilities in His Kingdom.

The second point to note is that not only has God chosen to give responsibility to His people, but through the administration of His people He has chosen to declare His wisdom to the principalities and powers. Let me explain more fully. God has taken fallen man, saved and redeemed him, and then placed him in His government, to use man against the very powers that brought about his downfall. Having once been the enemies of God, we are now used to attack those powers in the heavenlies. Of course, it could only come about through the cross of Christ, but what a tremendous turn around! God completely turns the tables on Satan and his host. They destroyed man's perfection, but now God takes and uses redeemed man to destroy the strongholds of Satan. How like God to bring victory out of defeat!

Jesus said to His disciples: 'Behold I have given you authority to tread upon serpents and scorpions, and over all the power of the enemy and nothing shall injure you' (Luke 10:19). We recognise immediately that the serpent stands for Satan, but scorpions equally stand for demonic powers. Here is another staggering statement, in that Jesus is giving authority to His followers to actually be able to place satanic forces under our feet, without being harmed. God isn't simply putting all enemies under the feet of Jesus, He is doing it through the Church – by the very people who were once under Satan's control. What a God and what a salvation!

For what purpose is this authority to tread on serpents and scorpions given to the disciples? We have already seen that it is a declaration of God's wisdom. Secondly, it is a means of completing Christ's victory by destroying the strongholds of Satan, and assisting God in bringing all enemies under the feet of Christ. What a privilege to be co-workers with God! Thirdly, we need to understand that this is part of the strategy linked with the proclamation of the gospel. When Paul spoke about the armour and the necessity of prayer for the saints, he then adds 'and pray on my behalf, that utterance may be given to me in the opening of my mouth, to make known with boldness the mystery of the gospel' (Ephesians 6:19). In other words, part of wrestling in prayer, is not just to defend ourselves and other Christians against Satan's attacks, but to create openings for the gospel. It means destroying the enemy's hold on the lives of men and women. We have already seen how praying for good government is related to the gospel and people coming to a saving knowledge of Christ. We have noted, too, how in Korea, with the powers of darkness defeated in prayer, there is a tremendous opening for the gospel, with thousands being won for Christ. So, we need to grasp that prayer and spiritual warfare is all part of the work of proclaiming the gospel of Christ.

In that connection, let us consider the statement of Jesus

in Matthew 12. In the passage, He had been accused of casting out demons by the prince of demons. He maintains that it is the complete opposite to their conclusions; it is, in fact, a demonstration of the Kingdom of God. He adds then this important point, 'How can anyone enter the strong man's house and carry off his property, unless he first binds the strong man? And then he will plunder his house' (v. 29). Remember, this is spoken against the background of Jesus casting a demon out of a man's life, as an assault on Satan's kingdom. Therefore, the clear implication is that if we are going to plunder Satan's household, we have first to bind Satan. If we are going to bring men and women out of the Kingdom of darkness, Satan (or the appropriate spirit) must first be bound, then people are free to respond to Christ. That is true of individuals or a nation. We need to pray for individuals until we receive authority to bind the demonic powers, then they can respond to Christ; or, as in Korea, we need to pray until we come to the position where the strong man over a nation can be bound.

We forget this in evangelism in Britain today. The spiritual climate in our country is not conducive to evangelism. I am not saying that we should not preach the gospel or that we should wait for a more opportune moment; what I am saying is that prayer is the essential preparation for evangelism. I believe the reason why so many people came to Christ in the Mission England and Mission to London crusades was because of the level of prayer offered to God. Even then, one would hardly start to describe these missions in terms of revival. We have to fight all the way in prayer, wrestling against the powers of darkness, and binding the strong man. In that way we can begin to change the spiritual climate of our nation.

What does it mean to bind the strong man? The Greek word for binding is used in a number of ways. It is used in the sense of tying up donkeys, bundles of corn, or prisoners. It is particularly in binding a prisoner that we talk of binding the strong man. He is bound so that he is powerless to act or harm those who would plunder his house.

There is a similar statement about binding in Matthew 16:18,19. Peter has just confessed that Jesus is the Messiah (Christ), the Son of the living God. Jesus replies to this by saying, 'You are Peter, and upon this rock I will build My church; and the gates of Hell shall not overpower it. I will give you the keys of the kingdom of heaven; and whatever you shall bind on earth shall have been bound in heaven, and whatever you shall loose on earth shall have been loosed in heaven.'

There are many who respond with fear to these lines, feeling that it gives something approaching papal authority to Peter. Just a cursory glance at the rest of the New Testament shows us that this is not the case. I have no difficulty understanding that, in a sense, Peter's ministry was foundational, for Paul says in Ephesians 2:20 that the Church is 'built upon the foundation of the apostles and prophets.' Peter is just one of the foundation stones as is shown in the Book of Revelation (21:14), although the real foundation that is laid, is Christ.

The most glorious part of these verses in Matthew is that 'the gates of Hell shall not overpower it.' It's strange how Satan has twisted our thinking. It is not the Church that is under attack, but the gates of Hell. When a town was attacked, the most vulnerable part was the gates. The gates of Hell are not going to stop the Church breaking in and destroying the strongholds of Satan. Satan has fooled us into thinking we are the ones under siege, so consequently we have gone on the defensive, instead of the offensive.

There is, however, another aspect to the matter of the gates of Hell. The gates of the city was the place where the court sat. When Boaz was approached as a redeemer to recover Naomi's land, and to marry Ruth, he took the matter to the elders at the entrance of the gates of Bethlehem. Therefore, it could be that Jesus was saying that the council of Hell would not prevail against the Church. Whichever concept one uses it implies victory for the Church.

That note of triumph is further emphasised, when Jesus said, 'I will give you the keys of the kingdom of Heaven;

and whatever you shall bind on earth shall have been bound in heaven, and whatever you shall loose on earth shall have been loosed in heaven.' Keys speak to us of locking or unlocking doors or locking up people. It is used four times in this way in the Book of Revelation. In the first case Jesus says that He has 'the keys of death and of Hades' (1:18). Obviously, Jesus has authority over death and Hades and was able to control them. The second reference (3:7) is to Jesus having the key of David and that when He opens, no one will shut the door, but when He shuts it no one can open it. Because the Church at Philadelphia had been faithful, Jesus was going to set before them an open door and even the powers of darkness would not prevent it opening. In the third reference (9:1), a key is used to release the powers of darkness in a final act of judgement upon the earth, but in Revelation 20:1, a key is used by the angel so that Satan can be bound for a thousand years.

We can deduce from this that when Jesus gave to Peter the keys of the Kingdom of Heaven, he was giving authority to lock up or to set free. This is further emphasised by the words 'bind' and 'loose'. We have already seen too that Satan was 'bound' with the use of a key for a thousand years. A jailor has authority to lock up or to release prisoners and in a similar way, Peter is given authority to bind or to set free.

There is another important point to note in this passage. The tenses are very crucial to our understanding and are brought out best in the NAS version. Jesus says, 'Whatever you *shall* bind on earth *shall have been* bound in heaven.'[1] It has to be bound in Heaven first, then we can bind on earth. If we refer back to the reference in Revelation 9:1, we could not bind those powers of darkness if God is releasing them. That would be to work against God, and we could find ourselves as powerless as the sons of Sceva, who, in trying to cast out demons in the name of Paul and Jesus, were violently attacked (Acts 19:14f).

Paul had often dealt with demonic activity. He had, for instance, cast out a spirit of divination from a fortune-teller

[1]Some copies of the NAS do not have this wording.

at Philippi, yet there came a situation where God gave him no authority to deal with an enemy attack. He tells us that he was given a thorn in the flesh, which came as a messenger of Satan to buffet him. A lot of people puzzle over what Paul's thorn in the flesh was really about, yet scripture gives us the clues. In the first place, the phrase 'thorns in the eyes' was used in Joshua 23:13 where the Israelites were warned that if they did not drive out the other nations from the Promised Land, they would be a thorn in the eyes. The enemy, if not dealt with properly, would be a painful irritant.

Secondly, the word in the Greek for messenger is usually translated 'angel'. An angel of Satan is clearly a demonic spirit which was giving Paul a bit of a battering. It would seem that the attacks came in the form of weakness, insults, distresses, persecutions and difficulties (see 2 Corinthians 12:10).

Paul tells how he asked the Lord three times to rid him of this attack. God's answer was plain, 'My grace is sufficient for you, for power is perfected in weakness.' The apostle discovered that there were two reasons why God did not remove the attack. First of all, Paul had received some amazing revelations from God. Great apostle though he was, he was still in danger of becoming proud. God removed just a little of Paul's protection, so that the enemy could attack. There's nothing like a thorn in the flesh to reduce an inflated head back to size! It's most humbling to find there are situations that are beyond us. Secondly, God was teaching Paul that His power was shown best in human weakness. Perhaps this is most clearly seen when Paul and Silas were thrown into prison. The enemy causes them to be persecuted and wrongly accused, but with backs bleeding, they sing praises to God at midnight. That's enough to convince a hardened jailor that these men have really got something, and then, after an earth-shaking experience, the jailor is saved and baptised together with his family – all within a few hours! How's that for God demonstrating His power in weakness?

The main point of recalling this incident is that Paul

could not bind this evil spirit. God had allowed the activity of the enemy for a purpose. Without God's authority, Paul was powerless to deal with the angel of Satan.

Another instance that illustrates this point is in Judges chapter 9. There was a conspiracy between Abimelech, a son of Gideon, and the people of Shechem, to kill his seventy brothers, and become, in effect, their king. Obviously, this met with God's disapproval, so 'God sent an evil spirit between Abimelech and the men of Shechem; and the men of Shechem dealt treacherously with Abimelech.' As a consequence war broke out between them, resulting in the destruction of the city and the death of Abimelech. God used an evil spirit in this incident to divide and destroy as part of His judgement. How foolish it would be, if we were in the situation, to try to bind that evil spirit; we would have no authority from God, and would probably end up flattened by the demonic power. Yet, Christians persist in binding the enemy without understanding the principles on which God works. If God has sent an evil spirit as part of His judgement, then the only way that spirit can be stopped is by first repenting, and then asking God to remove the demonic power.

We have already covered Jesus' statement to Peter (in Matthew 16:18,19), but just two chapters later all the disciples are addressed along the same lines. Again Jesus tells them that they can bind on earth what has first been bound in Heaven. Then He adds these words: 'If two of you agree on earth about anything that they may ask, it shall be done for them by My Father in Heaven', concluding with the promise that 'where two or three have gathered together in My name, there I am in their midst' (Matthew 18:19,20). Jesus is showing that if only two are praying together, He is present, and if there is true agreement on a matter, together with Him, then God will grant the request. I do not think we can separate the agreement of the two people with Jesus being present. Obviously, if two people agree on a matter and Jesus would not approve of it, I do not believe their request could then be granted. Because these two verses are in the context of binding and loosing, it is as if Jesus is saying, 'Where only two or three of you are praying, and there is the witness of the Spirit that what you ask is right, then not only will your requests be granted, but you will have authority from Heaven to bind and loose.' There needs to be, however, that witness of the Spirit before we can bind the enemy.

Why does Jesus talk about two or three people being gathered together? It is important to understand that there are times when we can only bind and loose with others present. It seems that there needs to be a minimum of two people. There can then be the witness between them, by the Holy Spirit, that God has actually given them authority to bind the enemy. If the enemy attacks us, as individuals we can rebuke or bind the powers of darkness, for we have authority over our own lives. A father can rebuke the enemy over his family, because he has authority over his family, and a pastor has authority over his church. Of course, we need to know that God is giving us authority in these cases. On bigger issues, however, we need the witness of others that it is right to proceed.

There are times when we may need to pray for some considerable time, even weeks, or years before we may receive the authority from God to bind demonic forces at work in our nation. We may be able to come against the enemy sometimes, in a limited way, but some demonic powers have such a grip, or we are under such judgement from God, that it will take a long time to make the final breakthrough. Remember, how in Daniel's case, he was praying for three weeks before the archangel Michael finally entered into the battle, releasing the angel from the hold of the prince of Persia. All too frequently we find people, as soon as they start praying, beginning to bind the enemy. We often need to confess first the sin of the Church or the nation, before God will give us such authority. Even then we might be so under the judgement of God that we do not have heaven's permission to bind the enemy in this particular instance. When, however, we do receive God's authority, then having bound the powers of darkness and released people from their grip, there is an immediate or a definite change in the situation.

Some years ago, as a church, we were praying about the Unification Church, commonly called the Moonies. (Moon claimed to be the Messiah and to have succeeded where Jesus had failed. Along with most evangelical Christians we believed him to be a false messiah.) We were, at that time, planning a tent crusade when suddenly a Moonie joined our meetings. He seemed interested and open, but we were a little concerned lest he reported to the Unification Church that we were planning to hold a crusade. The Moonies had infiltrated some of the churches on Merseyside and even tried to infiltrate the counselling system at a David Watson Christian Festival in Liverpool. In the light of this, we did not want them to repeat the operation with us, so we began praying about their activities. God gave us a specific word that they would not come near our tent crusade or fire a single shot in our direction. However, we were still concerned about their influence in Liverpool. As we continued to pray about this matter over two or three successive weeks, we felt that God gave us authority to bind the deceiving spirit behind this cult, but only as far as Merseyside was concerned.

God then enlarged our praying to seek Him for the complete defeat of the Moonies in Britain. Eventually, having prayed over a period of time we were aware that God was giving us authority to bind this deceiving spirit over the whole nation. It was interesting that as we began to pray about the matter nationwide, the Daily Mail published a series of articles about the brain-washing activities of the Moonies. Then followed a long court case, with the Unification Church accusing the Daily Mail of libel. Eventually the paper was cleared of the charge, having successfully proved their point in the courts. As a result, the Unification Church moved their headquarters out of London and on to the Continent. God had heard our prayers, together with many others who were praying around the country. He had given us the witness from heaven to bind this demonic system and the spirit behind it.

There are those who rebuke or bind Satan himself. It is, however, very unlikely that we would be attacked directly by Satan. Jesus had a direct encounter with him, but Jesus' ministry was so important that it demanded the highest attention at enemy command. We are much more likely to encounter evil spirits, principalities or world rulers. Therefore our rebuke ought to be directed at those particular powers involved in the situation, rather than Satan.

It is also worth remembering, as in the case of Daniel, that when we are engaged in spiritual warfare, the angels are also involved in the battle. The angels are 'ministering spirits, sent out to render service for the sake of those who will inherit salvation' (Hebrews 1:14). David wrote: 'The angel of the Lord encamps around those who fear Him, and rescues them' (Psalm 34:7). In Rhodesia, before it became Zimbabwe, there were terrorists who saw angels protecting Christians and in some cases it led to the conversion of some of those rebels.

Authority to bind and loose is a tremendous responsibility, but a real privilege. It involves acting in the name of Jesus and therefore, only with his expressed approval. If, however, we fail to move into this area of responsibility, we allow the enemy to take ground from us, but if we are waging war and using the authority that God would so often invest in us, then we can begin to win back the territory from the powers of darkness. For too long, we have allowed Satan to make all the advances. Now is the time for us to rise up and take the Land!

9

Persist in Prayer

One quality that is often lacking among Christians is perseverance. Somehow, even in church circles, we have to be always finding something new, spectacular and sensational. In many ways we pander to the flesh. Yet in Scripture there is an emphasis on endurance.

Colossians 4:2 (RSV) says, 'Continue in prayer, being watchful in it with thanksgiving.' The Greek word means 'to continue steadfastly' and was used by one historian to describe a state of siege. Other versions translate this word as 'devote' yourself to prayer, but certainly it contains the idea of persistence. In Acts 2:42, we see that the early church devoted themselves to prayer. Today's church may devote itself to many things, but prayer is not among its priorities, generally speaking. We need to rediscover this devotion to prayer.

In considering Paul's instruction to the Colossians, the concept of a siege has much to offer. We have already seen that we are involved in a warfare. That is rarely a pushover. In the Falklands, the marines and the paratroopers yomped over miles and miles of marshy land in an effort to take the Argentine forces by surprise. They expected a full-frontal attack on Port Stanley from the sea – not across such impossible terrain. Such warfare demanded the persistence of every soldier. In the First World War a few feet were gained at a time across the muddy trenches of the battle field.

Where churches do have prayer meetings, it often becomes a case of around the world in eighty minutes, but preferably in a lot less time than that! All sorts of matters are covered from missionaries in Peru, to Auntie Gerty's goitre – not that it is wrong to pray for these things. The trouble is that we so rarely enter into spiritual warfare and persist in prayer. Praise God, things are beginning to change, but we need to persevere in prayer until we batter down the gates of Satan's strongholds. One of the requirements of wrestling is persistence, but when do we show the same qualities in wrestling against principalities and powers?

Paul adds another aspect to our praying when he says, 'Continue steadfastly in prayer, being watchful in it . . .' Literally the Greek means 'be awake'. A guard on sentry duty is no use at all in protecting a city if he sleeps, neither is a soldier who falls asleep in the middle of a battle; yet we as Christians have been sleeping while Satan has robbed us of our territory. The advance that Islam has made, together with the inroads of Satan worship, witchcraft, transcendental meditation, pornography, spiritualism and secularism, has happened largely because the Church has been asleep. I believe we need to say very clearly to the Church in Britain, 'For God's sake, wake up, before it's too late!'

Part of the trouble is that our enemy has lulled us into a false sense of security, and given us a warped view of tolerance. We are told that there is nothing wrong with other religions; we just find God through different paths. Paul describes the other gods as demons, and Jesus condemns the Church in Pergamum because there are those who are teaching that people should feel free to eat food sacrificed to idols and to commit acts of immorality. Jesus calls them to repent or He will make 'war against them' with the sword of His mouth. The Church at Thyatira is rebuked because it has tolerated the same teaching from a false prophetess. The Son of God declares that He has given her time to repent; now He will bring sickness and death upon her. Every time church leaders participate in pagan festivals, they are as guilty as the Church of Thyatira. Immorality is often allowed to go unchecked, with even clergymen being guilty and not being removed from office by the bishops, but simply transferred to other parishes. We are told that we must be loving and tolerant. No wonder we have lost a holy zeal to destroy the demonic strongholds when tolerance has been so distorted.

We need, therefore, not only to persist in prayer but to be watchful. Jesus told His disciples to watch and pray, lest they enter into temptation. We must be watchful as to the strategy of the enemy, then persist in prayer to the point of victory. In Paul's famous passage about wrestling against principalities and powers, he ends by saying, *'Be on the alert* with all *perseverance* and *petition* for all the saints' (Ephesians 6:18).

We can see this persistence in prayer prior to Pentecost. Scripture records how during those ten days between the ascension and Pentecost the believers devoted themselves to prayer. No wonder there was an outpouring of the Holy Spirit. However, they did not give up after that event, for we read that the 3,000 who were converted at Pentecost devoted themselves to prayer (Acts 2:42). It is not surprising that the Church continued to know the power of God.

When Peter was imprisoned and awaiting trial before Herod, 'prayer . . . was being made fervently by the church to God' (Acts 12:5). They obviously continued to pray about this particular matter, and as a result, God laid on one of those lovely, little surprises to delight the people of God. He acted in a way that was above all they could ask or think, by causing an angel to release him. When Peter turned up at the prayer meeting, they couldn't believe it! The church had persisted in prayer to the point of victory, but we do that all too infrequently.

One is impressed with the story of Joshua when he attacked Ai. After the Israelites had dealt with the sin of Achan, they moved against the city the second time. Then God spoke to Joshua saying, 'Stretch out the javelin that is in your hand towards Ai, for I will give it into your hand.' The narrative ends by stating, 'Joshua did not withdraw his hand with which he stretched out the javelin until he had utterly destroyed all the inhabitants of Ai' (Joshua 8:18,26). He saw the conflict through to completion.

Moses, likewise, persisted as Israel fought the Amalekites. When he lifted up his hands in prayer, then Israel prevailed, but when he grew weary, then the Amalekites began to gain the advantage. You may remember, that it was only when he was supported by Aaron and Hur that victory was finally accomplished. So often we grow weary in the battle and do not persevere to victory, thus the enemy wins the final victory. It is worth noting that, great intercessor though Moses was, he needed the support of others. (Here is a practical example of two or three gathering together, in spiritual warfare, in the name of the Lord.)

Many readers of this book will be aware of the problems that Liverpool has experienced in recent years. Several years ago, at the time of the local government elections, we felt that the city was under God's judgement and we would get the councillors we deserved. A few years earlier, Liverpool had been a centre of Satan worship with people coming from Scotland to the city for their occultic worship. As the city became increasingly dominated by the powers of darkness, its people had become rebellious and defiant. We knew that frequently God gives to a militant and rebellious people, militant and rebellious leaders. We also felt that, perhaps, God was allowing the militants to gain power to reveal the real nature of their aims.

We came before God seeking His mercy upon the City of Liverpool and the surrounding district. We confessed the sin of the area, and the sin of the Church, including its own rebelliousness and prayerlessness. We asked that God would begin to deal with the militants, especially as, by now, the council had openly become more militant and was defiant of national government. The city had become a tool to express Marxist policies, and a means of seeking to bring the nation under Marxist control.

As part of this battle with central government, the council refused to set a legal budget and was prepared to allow the city to become bankrupt in order to force the hand of

Parliament. At that point, schools were beginning to close down because they ran out of heating oil and materials, social services were in danger of grinding to a halt, and 30,000 council workers were about to be made redundant.

We had been praying about the situation during those months of increasing crisis. We prayed that God would reveal the extent of intimidation that might have been going on; expose any fraudulent activity; and the way in which supporters of Militant Tendency had been put into key jobs. As the crisis loomed nearer, Derek Hatton, the deputy leader of the council, and one of the most militant councillors, boasted that the Labour council would never be divided. The Guardian reported Derek Hatton as saying, 'They can pray all they like, but there is no chance whatsoever of the Liverpool group splitting on this major issue. We will stand firm. We will not do Thatcher's dirty work for her and we will win.'

We felt that it was an open challenge to God and needed to be taken up in prayer. In fact we had already called a day of prayer and fasting in our Fellowship as the crisis loomed. We know that others were praying in Liverpool on that October day in 1985, including leaders of Lydia, and other IFB groups around the country were mobilised to pray. By the time the day had finished we felt that God had given us authority to declare that the council would be defeated and divided. In fact we concluded our prayer time outside the town hall singing 'Jesus is Lord' and prophesying the defeat of Militant and the division of the council.

During the evening of that day of prayer and fasting, unbeknown to us, Neil Kinnock was making his strongest attack on Militant Tendency and the Liverpool councillors. This was followed up later by the National Executive of the Labour Party organising an enquiry into the Liverpool district Labour Party. In the meantime the councillors were forced to back down from bankrupting the City by borrowing money from Swiss bankers. The police also announced that they had interviewed Derek Hatton, and had passed on a report to the Director of Public Prosecutions.

The tide of events continued to flow swiftly against the Liverpool councillors. The Labour Party enquiry found damning evidence against the Militant Tendency supporters in terms of intimidation and irregularities in the conduct of the Liverpool District Labour Party and it was consequently banned from meeting, by the National Executive of the Labour Party. Then there was an attempt among the Labour councillors to have Derek Hatton removed as deputy leader of the council.[1] Although this failed, the split that he predicted would never happen, had actually begun to take place. God was answering our prayers. Then just over a week later on Tuesday, 4th March, 1986, the High Court found the councillors guilty of misconduct in not setting a legal budget, and consequently banned them from holding office as councillors for five years.

I have told this story because it illustrates how we need to persist in prayer. Our prayer battle concerning the council must have been over a period of five years and certainly meant we had to persist in prayer before we saw the final victory. We may need to come back to a matter time and time again before we see the answers we would like. That is why Scripture is clear that we need to persist in prayer.

---

[1]Derek Hatton was in fact sacked from his job with Knowsley Council on 22nd July 1986.

10

By Few or Many

In the days when Israel was being oppressed by the Philistines, Jonathan was grieved that the garrison of the Philistine army was situated at Michmash. Without telling his father (perhaps he considered that his father didn't have sufficient faith for the venture) Jonathan went with his armour-bearer to attack the enemy encampment. Aware that they were only two against an enemy stronghold, Jonathan encouraged his solitary supporter by saying, 'the Lord is not restrained to save by many or by few' (1 Samuel 14:6). When they received the right sign, as being confirmation from God to attack, they went up against the garrison. Within a short space of time they had killed 20 men, and the resulting confusion and chaos brought further destruction to the enemy and even encouraged some of the Israelites who had been living among the Philistines to fight against them. Other Israelites who had gone into hiding now joined the battle, so that in the end the Philistines were thoroughly routed.

Israel's history confirms that God is able to save by the few. Gideon's army was reduced in size so that the nation might understand that it was God who was giving them the victory. The same is true in spiritual warfare. Moses with the assistance of Aaron and Hur, prevailed in prayer to save the nation. We have already seen that Jesus talks about just two or three praying together, with the implication that they can bind the enemy. On the other hand, how much better when a whole nation turns to God as when Jehoshaphat called the nation to prayer and fasting. How I long to see the Church of God in Britain really seeking God's face.

While that may be our desire, it is encouraging to note that again and again it has been one solitary figure kneeling in prayer that has brought God's intervention. It may be Moses fasting and praying on Sinai that saves a nation from God's judgement, or, on another occasion, Nehemiah is found mourning over the charred walls of Jerusalem, praying that God would again restore the city. Later in time, we are confronted with Daniel confessing the sin of his nation, acknowledging that God has dealt justly with them, but praying that God would restore the glory of the temple and the splendour of Jerusalem. How much was accomplished by Paul praying in prison for individuals and churches? God alone knows the travailing in prayer. Paul tells the Colossians that Epaphras is 'always labouring earnestly for you in his prayers, that you may stand perfect and fully assured in all the will of God' (Colossians 4:12). Again, only eternity will reveal the outcome of those prayers. Dwight Moody declared that 'every great movement of God can be traced to one kneeling figure.'

God, Himself, shows the importance of just one person praying, when, as we have already seen, He says, 'I searched for *a man* among them who should build up the wall and stand in the gap before Me for the land that I should not destroy it; but I found no-one' (Ezekiel 22:30). Again Isaiah records that 'the Lord saw, and it was displeasing in His sight that there was no justice. And He saw that there was no man, and was astonished that there was no one to intercede' (Isaiah 59:15,16). On this occasion God intervened, but clearly He is looking for one person to intercede.

When Joshua was advanced in years, he addressed the nation and reminded them of what God had done. He encouraged them to be obedient to the Lord, lest they should perish from the Land. Then he declared: 'No man has stood before you to this day. One of your men puts to flight a thousand, for the Lord your God is He who fights for you, just as He promised' (Joshua 23:9,10). Obedience and trust had brought them victory after victory in the

Promised Land, even to the extent of one man overcoming a thousand. God specialises in overwhelming odds.

It may be worth pausing for a moment to recognise that the battles of the Old Testament are not just stories of war, but spiritual conflict. So many of the nations and tribes that fought against Israel took their gods into battle with them. When David fought against the Philistines at the Valley of Rephaim, they gathered up the Philistine idols and burnt them. The demonic forces involved with these idols were trying to prevent the purposes of God. This was also true of the Amalekites who confronted Israel soon after leaving Egypt. We have seen that victory for the children of Israel was only achieved by prayer. As a result of this assault on Israel, God declared that He would blot out the memory of the Amalekites from under heaven.

When Joshua stated that, with God's help, 'one could fight a thousand', he wasn't talking about the logistics of war; he was talking about spiritual warfare. When Moses, Aaron and Hur prayed, the real conflict was in the heavenlies. As Daniel prayed, angels and archangels became involved in the heavenly struggle. When Israel was obedient to God, then one could overcome a thousand. God gave a similar assurance, through Moses, of overwhelming victory for Israel if they were obedient to God. God said that part of the blessing of obedience was 'five of you will chase a hundred, and a hundred of you will chase ten thousand, and your enemies will fall before you by the sword (Leviticus 26:8). God's mathematics are somewhat surprising, and not what we would logically expect. By normal arithmetic 100 should chase 2,000 (not 10,000) if 5 can chase 100!

I do not want to press the conclusions of the above equations too far, but we can clearly say that if we are in the minority, it is no problem to God. One person praying can put strong forces to rout. A few involved in a battle can accomplish great things. It would seem, however, that if the numbers involved in the battle are increased, the effect can be even more devastating. There are some forces of darkness that really require a rising up of greater numbers, so that we can win the victory against overwhelming odds. How are we going to break-through against the principality of Islam or Communism? The Church in Korea, by their prayers, have withstood that principality of Communism and thousands in Yongi Cho's church flock to their prayer mountain every week to carry on the battle for their land. We, too, can have confidence before God no matter how great the hoards of Islam, Hinduism, or Communism. As Jehoshaphat prayed to God when three mighty armies were converging on his tiny army, so we can pray, 'We are powerless before this great multitude who are coming against us; nor do we know what to do, but our eyes are on you' (2 Chronicles 20:12).

The purpose of this chapter is to show that numbers don't matter with God, and He accomplishes so much through individuals. As Jonathan said, 'The Lord is not restrained to save by many or by few.' Yet, one can't help feel that if God's people stood up as an army to wrestle against principalities and powers, then the victories would increase out of all proportion to our size. Don't be discouraged by the smallness of your group praying for Albania or Aberdeen, Mongolia or Manchester. God will break down the strongholds of the enemy through your prayers. My appeal is to the Church, to rise up and move heaven and earth by its strong, fervent intercession. It's time for the Church of God to be on the move and march out in the power of our God.

11

David's Mighty Men

In any army, there are always those men who have different
abilities and specialities. All are required in the warfare.
The infantry, paratroopers, engineers, commandos and
tank crews are all essential in a successful campaign, and
so within the army of God, we need people with different
functions. The prophet is able to warn of impending
danger, or the possibilities of God's judgement. Those with
the discernment of spirits may recognise just what demonic
forces are at work. There are those who are strong in
intercession; while still others give encouragement when
our spirits flag.

David was surrounded by men with differing abilities
and effectiveness. I am always encouraged and challenged
when I read 1 Chronicles 12 concerning David's mighty
men. For instance, we read in verse 8 that from the Gadites
there came 'mighty men of valour, men trained for war,
who could handle shield and spear.' Men of valour are vital
in any army. Those who are fearful are not fit for fighting.
You may remember that Gideon's army was reduced drasti-
cally in size when God said that the warriors who were
fearful should go home. It is interesting that when Moses
gave instruction concerning the army, he said, 'The officers
shall speak to the people, and they shall say, "Who is the
man that is afraid and fainthearted? Let him depart and
return to his house, so that he might not make his brothers'
heart melt like his heart" ' (Deuteronomy 20:8).

It was this very matter of fear which caused the Israelites
to wander in the wilderness for forty years. Of course,

there were many other factors involved, such as unbelief, disobedience and hardness of heart, but the governing factor was fear. The spies reported back that the cities were too well fortified, and the people were too tall and strong to be defeated. That report made the people's resolution and strength melt away with fear (Deuteronomy 1:28). No wonder Scripture repeats the command over 350 times, 'Do not fear.'

To off-set this tendency towards fear, in any army, we need men of valour who will show real courage in the face of the enemy. Gideon was addressed by God as 'O valiant warrior' (Judges 6:12). It always strikes me as being very amusing that God should address him in this way. This man is so afraid of the Midianites that he is winnowing wheat in a wine press. That is the most stupid place to sift the corn from the chaff. What is required is an exposed spot so that the wind can blow away the chaff, whereas a wine press is dug down into the ground. Then God commands Gideon to destroy the altar of Baal, and so, because he is afraid of the men of the city, he sets out, under the cover of darkness, to demolish the demonic structure. This is the man that God has chosen to destroy the Midianites, and is addressed by the Almighty as 'a mighty man of valour' (AV). Before the chapter closes, however, God turns this timid and insignificant man into a valiant warrior, as the Holy Spirit endues him with power. Praise God that He is able to turn people who, by nature, are fearful and timid, into men and women of courage and strength.

Let me emphasise, how important it is, in spiritual warfare, not to be fearful. If we are, we shall never really make any stand against the armies of Satan because we will be afraid of the repercussions. Kings, prophets, priests and pastors have lost their ministries because of fear. We are able to be men of valour through God's power. We do not need to fear the powers of darkness because 'greater is He who is in you than he who is in the world' (1 John 4:4).

The second thing that we discover about the Gadites in David's army was that they were 'trained for war.' The one thing the Church has failed in, is preparing men for war. We train preachers, evangelists, counsellors, pastors and to some extent people for the healing ministry, but there is very little training for spiritual warfare. Paul, however, talks about wrestling against principalities and powers, and demolishing the strongholds of the enemy, but we seem almost powerless before Satan and his host.

This book has been written in the hopes that others will learn to fight this war. It was in Prayer and Bible Weeks, under the leadership of Denis Clark, that I learnt what spiritual warfare was about. I saw others fighting this battle and began to fight alongside them, thus learning something of the art of war.

These warlike men from the tribe of Gad 'could handle shield and spear.' If we are to be effective in warfare, we need to be able to defend effectively, as well as attack. One of the favourite flaming missiles that the enemy uses is that of lies. We need to use the shield of faith to quench the power of such a deadly weapon. He tells us that we can never be forgiven for some particular sin, or God couldn't possibly use us, or God doesn't love us. All of these attacks sap our strength and confidence, but as we use the shield of faith to parry this deadly assault, believing what God has spoken, we are then able to stand firm against our adversary and go on the offensive.

We know that the sword of the Spirit is the Word of God. I believe that includes words of prophecy and the word of rebuke against demonic forces, as well as the words of Scripture. I am not in any way comparing prophecies and words of rebuke with the Scriptures, for they stand apart in their inspiration. When, however, the Spirit of God gives us words to utter against the enemy, the authority is of God, and becomes the cutting edge of the Spirit to destroy the works of the enemy. God says through Hosea, 'I have hewn them in pieces by the prophets; I have slain them by the words of My mouth; and the judgements on you are like the light that goes forth' (Hosea 6:5). Of course, the Bible itself is so vital in our warfare. Jesus so skilfully demonstrated this by responding to Satan's attack, with the words of Scripture, saying each time, 'It is written . . .'

There was another group that joined David who came from the tribes of Benjamin and Judah. When David challenged them as to why they were joining him, the Holy Spirit fell on Amasai, one of their company, who said, 'We are yours, O David . . . peace to him who helps you; indeed your God helps you.' The Holy Spirit enabled them to see that God was no longer working in Saul's house and that authority was being switched to David. It was true that King Saul had received a new heart, and the Spirit had come upon him so that he prophesied, but the time came when God departed from Saul because of his disobedience. He lived on past blessings and died in rebellion. Unable to hear the voice of God any longer, he turned to witchcraft for his guidance. Amasai, however, together with his men, saw where God was at work, and joined forces with David.

We need the Spirit of God to show us where He is at work today. Yesterday's men, who live on their past reputation and past glories, will not build the Kingdom of God today. They need to be vitally in touch with God now, so as to know His direction. Those who start to build empires for themselves, rather than serving the Lord, will discover that God has moved on, having taken away His authority and given it to another.

There is one more group that particularly inspires me among David's mighty men; they were the descendants of Issachar. Their special contribution was that they 'understood the times, with the knowledge of what Israel should do.' I long for more of that sort of revelation and expertise. It is important for all of us involved in leadership to know what the people of God should be doing. We need to have our ears open to the Lord. We need to understand the times.

The Scriptures help us to understand the times, and the events that will take place in the last days. We know for instance, from 2 Thessalonians 2, that before the Lord returns, the apostasy must first take place, and the man of lawlessness will come. In fact, I wonder whether we have begun to approach the time of apostasy when we hear of church leaders denying essential doctrines such as the virgin birth, the divinity of Christ, the resurrection, and the efficacy of the cross. That same chapter says, 'You know what restrains him (the man of lawlessness) now, so that in his time he may be revealed.' There is a time to restrain this person, even by our praying, but at the appropriate time the man of lawlessness will come on the scene. There is no point in opposing him then, because he will come to power. We can pray for his eventual defeat, but God has a purpose in allowing this man to appear 'in order that they all may be judged who did not believe the truth.' Through the Antichrist those who have rejected the truth will be caught in a web of deception, so that there will clearly be a separation between the true and the false.

I remember, some years ago, we prayed that the Ayatollah Khomeni would never leave France and return to Iran. We were absolutely right in seeing the dangers of this man, long before the Iranian Revolution began. I don't think it was because we failed to pray sufficiently that he came to power. I believe that God had a purpose in allowing this man to bring about the Islamic Revolution. In Ezekiel 38 and 39, we read of the Gog and Magog War when Iran will come against Israel, together with other nations such as Russia, Ethiopia and Libya. Israel has never been at war with these nations, but Scripture states definitely that such a war will take place in the last days. I believe that places it in the near future, but until the Ayatollah came to power, Iran was one of Israel's most loyal supporters. All Israel's oil came from Iran.

Now the situation has completely changed and Khomeni has declared that once Iraq is defeated, he will march on Jerusalem to liberate that city from Israel's control. Yet God has said that Iran, together with the other nations, will be defeated on the mountains of Israel. Then all the nations will see God's glory (Ezekiel 39:4–8,21). Islam and Communism will be shown up for the false philosophies and demonic deceptions that they are. That is God's purpose and will probably result in many being delivered from Islam and Communism because of the disillusionment that will come upon them following such a defeat. Perhaps, therefore, if we had understood the times more fully (although we were aware that Persia [Iran] would come against Israel some day), we would not have prayed against the purposes of God.

In spiritual warfare we need this sort of insight. We need to know how far we can pray and resist the enemy. Eventually there will be a Godless confederation of states under the Antichrist. We can stand against him until that moment when God says, in effect, 'I am now allowing him to usurp power.' We can pray for his downfall, but we cannot pray against him ever appearing. We need, therefore, to understand the times.

Finally, Scripture says of David's mighty men that 'all these being men of war, who could draw up in battle formation, came to Hebron with a perfect heart, to make David king over all Israel.' There are three important points here. The first is that they knew their position in battle. They were a disciplined army, all taking up their proper battle stations. For too long the Church has been disjointed and fragmented. We need to move together as a unity under God-given leadership. We need to know how to relate to one another, especially in terms of spiritual warfare. We need to be able to alert other warriors when the enemy is attacking our territory such as when ungodly legislation is being introduced in Parliament, or major occultic meetings are taking place. In Intercessors For Britain, we jokingly say that we need an FBI in IFB!

Secondly, these men of war had 'a perfect heart.' If ever there was a time when Christians needed a perfect heart, it is now. We have so much impurity, jealousy, greed, selfishness and pride controlling our lives – to say nothing of materialism. We need a perfect heart where the Holy Spirit has brought about His glorious sanctification.

These men were motivated by one thing; they wanted to make David king over all Israel. How we need to lay aside our self-interest, our empire-building, and our jealousy of other people's ministries. All that matters is that through our intercession and warfare there is the strong plea 'Thy Kingdom come', which really becomes the burning desire of our hearts. It is not Methodism, Anglicanism, Pentecostalism, or even non-denominationalism that are important, but that Christ should be absolutely central. Our own position does not matter one iota, except that we fulfil our allotted task. The important issue is that we seek, with a perfect heart, to make Jesus truly King, both within His Church and finally over all the nations.

12

Strategy in War

In any war, we need a strategy to out-wit and out-gun the enemy. Although we may not out-wit Satan by human devices, we can wage war under the direction of God and thus be enabled to overcome the adversary. It is important that we come under the Captain of the Lord of Hosts just as Joshua did before attacking Jericho, because our own efforts are doomed to failure.

In any strategy, we must not overlook our own defences. I have already touched on the matter of our armour, as mentioned in Ephesians 6 and therefore do not intend to refer to this matter again, but take it for granted that we understand its importance. We need to make sure that we have left no loop-hole for Satan to exploit.

When the Israelites were defeated at Ai, God said to Joshua, 'You cannot stand before your enemies until you have removed the things under the ban from your midst.' They had been defeated because of disobedience and covetousness within the nation. It's important to make sure that our hearts are right in spiritual warfare.

We have also noted that when Paul talked in 2 Corinthians 10 about the weapons of our warfare not being of the flesh but mighty for the destruction of fortresses, he points out that they can only destroy those strongholds when their 'obedience is complete.' Disobedience to God means that, in a measure, we are siding with God's adversary. We do not have to be perfect first, but we do need to be cleansed from all sin before we can oppose the enemy. James makes the point very powerfully when he says,

'Submit to God. Resist the devil and he will flee from you' (James 4:7). Note the order: submission to God comes before resistance to the devil.

Another question we need to ask ourselves is, what place does the blood of Christ play in the warfare? Some Christians, as soon as they start to make a stand against Satan want to be covered by the blood of Christ. If we examine the scriptures carefully, the blood is always offered up to God for our cleansing and forgiveness. That is the case with the sacrifices offered on the altar in the Old Testament. Scripture says, 'without the shedding of blood there is no forgiveness' (Hebrews 9:22). In Hebrews 9:12f we see that Jesus entered by means of His blood into the holy place for our cleansing and redemption. At the time of Passover God 'passed over' the Jewish homes where the blood had been applied to the doorposts, but brought His judgement against the Egyptians. God, likewise, does not visit us in judgement because our Passover Lamb has been sacrificed and the blood has been applied to our lives.

The only place in Scripture when the blood is linked with Satan is in Revelation 12:11 where it says, 'They overcame him (Satan) because of the blood of the Lamb and because of the word of their testimony, and they did not love their life even to death.' The way in which the blood of Christ enables us to overcome Satan is that by faith in Christ and His sacrifice for our sin, the power of Satan is broken in our lives. When we confess our sin, then the blood of Jesus cleanses us from all unrighteousness, therefore Satan no longer has a loop-hole in our lives. That is the only way in which the blood of Christ gives a covering from Satan. The rest of the verse would confirm this because it talks about overcoming Satan by our testimony and not loving our lives. Isn't it by our confession of Christ as Lord (our testimony) and the fact that we lay down our lives to become His disciples that we find salvation and release from Satan's power? The blood of Christ, then, is for our forgiveness and cleansing. This breaks Satan's hold on our lives.

It is through the name of Christ that we really find

protection and authority to come against our adversary. Mark closes his gospel with the words of Jesus: 'In My name they (believers) will cast out demons.' In Jesus' prayer, which is recorded for us in John 17, we have these words: 'Holy Father, protect them (the disciples) by the power of Your name . . .' (v 11). We can see from this that it is God's name which gives protection for His people. This is confirmed in Proverbs 18:10: 'The name of the Lord is a strong tower; the righteous runs into it and is safe.' Again, it is worth noting, that it is the righteous who find God's protection. Therefore, when we are attacked by the enemy, we are able to rebuke him, in the name of the Lord, providing we are not giving the enemy an opening by our unrighteousness.

If we may summarise these matters; we need to confess our sin, then the blood of Jesus brings cleansing and leaves no unforgiven act of rebellion for Satan to exploit: we then have on the breastplate of righteousness. If we are walking in obedience, and have confessed all sin, then there is no opening for the devil and his aides. Consequently, we have His protection from any attempt of the enemy to harm us. Obviously, we may still come under attack by way of tempation, but we have the Lord's covering. There may, however, be times when we are aware of the enemy's vicious attacks, and need to take cover in the name of the Lord, and rebuke the enemy in Jesus' name. That is an authority the powers of darkness cannot overcome: such authority covers our lives because we are in Christ.

Our protection is important, but equally, in any war, we need a strategy for attack. You will find, however, that the cunningly devised plans of men are unnecessary. David always sought God before going into battle. In his first encounter with the Philistines after becoming king, he prayed, 'Shall I go up against the Philistines?' (2 Samuel 5:19) He didn't even assume it was right to go and fight them. I believe that we sometimes take on battles that God does not require us to fight. There are times when God gives over a nation to the enemy. Jeremiah was told not to pray for the nation, for their sin was so great (Jeremiah 7:16).

David was given permission to fight the Philistines but when, later, they regrouped, he still didn't assume that he had God's blessing to go against the enemy again. He sought God afresh and was given a different strategy this time. Instead of a full frontal attack, he was to circle around behind the enemy and wait until he heard a sound of marching in the balsam trees, for then he would know that the Lord had gone out to strike the Philistines.

There are a number of lessons to learn here. First of all, having defeated the enemy once does not guarantee a victory for all time. We may well have to fight the enemy on the same ground as before. Secondly, last week's directions are not sufficient for today. God wants us to rely on Him, not on our experience. Thirdly, God deliberately chose different tactics this time, partly to surprise the enemy but also so that David (and we) might learn to wait on Him for our orders. Perhaps the greatest thing to note is that God's army marched into battle. There is tremendous encouragement in knowing that God fights in the battle and His angels go before us. Hallelujah!

In those two encounters with the Philistines there was a different strategy for each battle. How different the strategy was that God gave to Joshua at Jericho. The priests and the people spent seven days circling the situation, and on that final day marched around it seven times. There is something of completion in the number seven, and a reminder to us that often we have to complete a thorough praying over, and around, a situation. I am sure that if some Christians had been there, before they were half way around, they would have started to bind the enemy and claim victory in the name of the Lord. Large strongholds take a great deal of circumventing in prayer, by a royal priesthood, before we move into attack and rout the enemy.

A friend of mine who led Intercessors for Rhodesia (as it was at that time) related to me how they were concerned about the powers of darkness around Bulawayo. It was at the beginning of 1978 that members of IFR felt God began to show them they needed to wage war against the Spiritualist Church in particular. About that time a Convention of Spiritualists was being held in Bulawayo, so the intercessors there began to pray against it. Soon afterwards, they received reports of how some people, who were going to the convention, turned back instead of entering the building.

During the following months that group of intercessors felt that they should increasingly fight against the spiritual forces behind spiritualism. God seemed to be confirming that they needed to conduct their campaign of attack in a similar way to Joshua's attack on Jericho. They decided that they needed to fast and pray over a full week, and carry on a complete 24-hour vigil with various people taking an hour, or half an hour, to pray. On the seventh day they felt that God had given them the victory and they noted the time on their watches – it was now 7 a.m. (They had gathered for prayer at 6 a.m. on that day.)

It wasn't very long before they started to receive news of three Spiritualists who became Christians on that final day of their prayer vigil. Then they heard of another three Spiritualists in South Africa who became Christians on that same day. Finally, news came that the Spiritualist Church, in Bulawayo, was condemned because of the state of the walls. After the necessary repairs, however, they were allowed to use the premises again. Members of Intercessors for Rhodesia began to pray again and repented for not persevering in prayer for the salvation of the Spiritualists. It was not very long before the local authorities announced that the building was to be demolished and the site used for an open air market. That group of interecessors were quite sure that what had taken place with the destruction of the building was only a sign of the greater destruction God had brought to the powers behind Spiritualism in Bulawayo. God knows the right strategy for the battle in hand.

One of the methods that God used to overthrow the enemies of Israel was that of confusion. When Gideon's soldiers shouted and broke the pitchers, the enemy was thrown into confusion, and in the darkness turned on one another. That was also true of the confederation of the three armies that marched against Jehoshaphat. Having pleaded with God for His help, God set ambushes so that the armies fought each other. There have been times when we have felt led to pray that God would throw the opponents of righteousness into total confusion.

We have already noted that we can ask God to allow an evil spirit into a situation to cause division and destruction. There may even be a place, sometimes, for delivering a person or movement over to Satan. We see that Paul told the Church in Corinth that he had done this so that a man who was guilty of gross immorality might know the power of the enemy in destroying his body. The purpose of this was that the man would then seek God's forgiveness and be restored. Again the Church in Rome is told not to associate with those who 'cause dissensions and hindrances contrary to the teaching' which they had received, so that Satan would soon be crushed under their feet (Romans 16:17,20). Discipline is part of the battle against the enemy.

There are times when we have prayed that God would reveal what was hidden. If the public learn the facts, often action can be taken to overcome the problem. Sometimes things come to light in surprising ways. Some years ago when we prayed about 'the Black Panther' and the 'Yorkshire Ripper' (men who were responsible for terrible crimes), the police caught the men whilst carrying out investigations into other more minor offences.

This is by no means an exhaustive list of the possibilities of waging war against the enemy, but it does show that we need to consider carefully the way in which we conduct the battle in which we are engaged. The fact remains that, if like Joshua we are under the Captain of the Lord's host, then we shall be led to adopt the right strategy for that particular battle. God is the master tactician and He knows the weakness of the enemy. David, although he was so small, was able to hit just the right place with a very meagre weapon, and overcome a foe who was immensely more powerful than he was. The victories that we win, through prayer, can be equally impressive, because it is our God who fights for us.

13

Moving Mountains

In October 1984, the situation concerning the miners' strike became very serious as the safety men, linked with the NACODS Union, threatened to come out on strike. Although these men were not yet on strike, some of the men were refusing to cross the picket-lines because of intimidation. The Coal Board felt that if these men were working, then they might be able to restart work at some of the mines. In order to bring pressure upon the safety workers to work normally, the Coal Board threatened to stop their pay if they refused to cross the picket-lines. (Until then all safety workers had been receiving their money.) The NACODS union, therefore, threatened an all-out strike. This would have had a serious effect on areas such as Nottingham which had refused to join the strike, as there had been no national ballot taken by the NUM. If, however, the safety men came out on strike, then no mine could be worked anywhere in Britain. That would have been a serious escalation of the strike!

Realising the seriousness of the situation, we prayed that the safety men would never strike. As the talks between the National Coal Board and NACODS got under way, we felt that the situation was crucial, as the whole strike could turn on the outcome of the talks. If they failed, then every pit in Britain would be idle. If they succeeded, then it would show to the members of the NUM that a solution could be found with the Coal Board, which could form a basis for an agreement with their union – if their leaders really wanted it.

Our IFB group met on the morning when the talks, between NACODS and the National Coal Board, were taking place. We felt God was encouraging us to pray that they would succeed. As we prayed, we sensed that God was giving victory, not only for those talks, but also for the end of the Miners' Strike. We felt so certain of this that we decreed the end of the strike. We were aware, however, that in making that decree, it was not going to be a sudden and dramatic end, but a slow return to work. Within two days it was announced that the Coal Board and NACODS had reached an agreement. Disillusionment began to set in among the NUM membership – especially as its leaders were not prepared to come to a similar agreement to the NACODS men. Then suddenly the dam began to break. All through November and December, men began to return. Pits, which had been closed for months, began to produce coal on a limited basis. More and more men returned to work, so that finally in February the strike ended, but still with no agreement between the NUM and the Coal Board.

It sounds very arrogant to say that we decreed the end of the strike, however, in Job 22:27,28 it says, 'You will pray to Him, and He will hear you; and you will pay your vows. You will also *decree* a thing, and it will be established for you.' Jesus also taught something similar when He said, 'Have faith in God. Truly I say to you, whoever says to this mountain, "Be taken up and cast into the sea," and does not doubt in his heart, but believes that what he says is going to happen, it shall be granted him' (Mark 11:22,23).

The context, in which Jesus uttered those words, was the cursing of the fig tree. Jesus had cursed the tree as a dramatic parable, that Israel had not produced the fruit that He was seeking. cf. Luke 13:1–8. (He also speaks of the revival of that fig tree, Israel, as being a sign that His return would be near.) The next day the disciples saw the fig tree withered and were amazed. Jesus then makes the statement quoted above. He is saying in effect, 'If you have faith in God, you can act in the same way just by giving a command, even to removing mountains.'

Was Jesus talking about literal mountains? Why not? It had been a literal tree that had been cursed and the apostle Paul talks about faith to remove mountains, yet how often would we need to move a literal mountain? On the other hand, Jesus chided the disciples for their lack of faith in failing to cast out a demon from a lad suffering with epilepsy. He then added, 'If you have faith as a mustard seed, you shall say to this mountain, "Move from here to there," and it shall move; and nothing shall be impossible to you' (Matthew 17:20). The 'mountain', or obstacle here, had been a demon that had not moved because of their lack of faith.

What are the principles that govern such an operation? Can we somehow screw up our faith and, by an act of determination, find the faith to remove obstacles or make decrees? The trouble is that we do not understand the nature of faith. Faith is not an act of our will, but a response to God's word. Romans 10:17 says, 'Faith comes from hearing, and hearing by the word of Christ.' From 1 Corinthians 12, we can see that faith is also a gift of the Holy Spirit. Faith, therefore, isn't an effort on our part; it is the response that we make to God's revelation through His word and the Holy Spirit. We can be blamed for our lack of faith when we do not respond to God's revelation, but we cannot conjure up faith by an effort of the will. Therefore, if we are going to have faith to remove mountains, we need some prompting and direction from God. We can then act in faith and cast out demons, remove obstacles, or make declarations that have the authority of God behind them.

We need to consider Jesus' statement in Mark 11 a little more, because the following verse says, 'Therefore I say to you, all things for which you pray and ask, believe that you have received them, and they shall be granted you' (v. 24). Some people have tried to summarise this in the pithy statement 'believe and receive'. Again, they would imply that an act of our will in believing something sufficiently, will bring about the desired result.

We need to understand, however, the principles involved in prayer. First of all, the matter of God's will is of primary importance. John tells us, 'This is the confidence which we have before Him, that, if we ask anything *according to his will*, He hears us. And if we know that He hears us in whatever we ask, we know that we have the requests which we have asked from Him' (1 John 5:14,15). Obviously the answers to our prayers depend on whether they fit in with God's will.

You may remember that Paul sought the Lord three times to have that messenger of Satan removed. It wasn't that he lacked faith, or that he failed to 'believe and receive'; it was that he was shown the purposes of God. God was going to demonstrate His power in Paul's weakness, enabling him to be victorious over the hardships he was facing.

There are other factors involved in receiving answers to our prayers. Jesus tells us, in John 15:7, that abiding in Him, and His word abiding in us, is an important element in receiving the requests of our heart. If we are in a close relationship with Him, then we will not pray for anything contrary to His will. Equally His Word will shape our prayers, helping to bring them into conformity with His will.

We shall see, in a later chapter, that sin will hinder our prayers and stop us receiving the answers we would like. Jesus presumably had this in mind, in the passage that we are considering in Mark 11, because He adds, 'And whenever you stand praying, forgive, if you have anything against anyone . . .'

We can see, therefore, that we cannot bring about these things by trying hard to believe. We have to pray according to God's will. Our relationship with Him is of paramount importance if we are to know His will, and so too is a knowledge of His Word. We need to recognise also, that sin will always hinder us from understanding the purposes of God.

Let us now return again to the statement of Jesus that we are considering. 'Truly I say to you, whoever says to the mountain, "Be taken up and cast into the sea," and does not doubt in his heart, but believes that what he says is going to happen, it shall be granted him. *Therefore* I say to you, all things for which you pray and ask, believe that you have received them, and they shall be granted you.' The action of moving mountains arises out of prayer and coming to the place of believing that God is giving you the answer. That means knowing His will, which is only discovered as we pray about it. Paul only discovered God's will about His thorn in the flesh, when he prayed about it. The disciples failed to cast out the demon, not only because of their lack of faith, but also because of their lack of prayer, for Jesus said, 'This kind cannot come out by anything but prayer' (Mark 9:29). The two go hand in hand; authority to command comes from a breakthrough in prayer.

You will see then, that when we decreed the end of the Miners' Strike, it was not presumption or arrogance on our part. We had been praying over the issue for months, trying to keep God's principles in mind as we considered His Word. We sought to keep our attitudes right by not allowing any personal feeling to creep in, and even confessing wrong attitudes towards Arthur Scargill or Ian McGregor. It was only at the point where we felt God was giving us the faith, that we dared to make any decree about the ending of the strike. It was not our action, but God's authority. We need to say, again and again, in every situation that I have related in this book, the glory is God's and not ours, yet He is wanting to work through His people. Although He has invested authority in us, we can only act in accordance with His will. He wants us to be in the mountain-moving business, but the faith and authority come from God. Let us pray that God will move some of those demonic mountains that dominate our land, and then look to Him for the moment when He will give us the faith. God wants mountain movers!

14

Fasting Turned to Feasting

I think most of us would like to find that our fasts are turned to feasts. I have to confess that I do not find fasting easy, neither do I find it easy to speak about it. You cannot preach on fasting unless you are willing to do it, and I always find a certain amount of conviction comes to me when I speak on the matter. The greatest hurdle I find is actually making the decision to fast on a certain day, or days. Once the decision is made, then I have no difficulty in following it through, but the battle comes in making the decision. Yet we have to realise how vital fasting is in spiritual warfare and intercession. By that I do not mean that every time we become involved in some spiritual battle or prayer concern we should fast – far from it, but there are times when it is essential.

In the Scriptures, we see that times of national crisis become times of fasting. They are almost too numerous to mention. Moses fasted and prayed at the time Aaron created the golden calf. The Israelites turned to prayer and fasting having suffered two defeats at the hands of the Benjaminites, before finally winning the victory at the third attempt. Jehoshaphat called the nation to prayer and fasting as a massive army from three nations converged on Judah's borders. Nehemiah, on hearing a report of the state of Jerusalem with its walls still in ruins, wept, fasted and prayed for the restoration of the city. Daniel fasted and prayed as he considered the seventy years exile predicted by Jeremiah, and then prayed that God would restore the nation.

Fasting is also linked with repentance. God spoke through Joel saying, 'Return to Me with all your heart, and with fasting, weeping, and mourning; and rend your heart and not your garments' (Joel 2:12). Joel then encourages the people to obey God by adding, 'Who knows whether He will not turn and relent, and leave a blessing behind Him . . . Blow a trumpet in Zion, consecrate a fast, proclaim a solemn assembly.' The prophet was aware that the nation had sinned and deserved God's judgement, but in turning to God in repentance, fasting and prayer, he was hoping that God would turn away from His anger and, in the end, bless them instead!

I believe in many ways, we as a nation, deserve the judgement of God. Indeed it is clear that we are experiencing a measure of judgement as God is allowing Satan to get a deeper grip upon our land. Yet if God's people will rise up and seek His face in fasting 'who knows whether He will not turn and relent and leave a blessing behind?'

We have already noted that God's promise to Solomon was: 'If my people humble themselves . . . and pray . . . I will heal their land.' Humbling oneself is often linked with fasting. David said in Psalm 35, 'I humbled my soul with fasting.' There is something about fasting, when entered into sincerely, that says in effect, 'God, I need your help. I can't cope with the situation; I need your intervention.'

There was an occasion when Ezra boasted to the king that they didn't need an army escort travelling with them for their protection, as God would keep them safe. Suddenly, he seems not only to have been confronted by his own words, but also by the dangers of the journey. He was too ashamed to ask the king for help after his statement of trust in God and now he wasn't quite so confident. He records, 'I proclaimed a fast there . . . that we might *humble* ourselves before our God to seek from Him a safe journey.' Perhaps he had felt he had been somewhat presumptuous in assuming that God would protect men, women and children on their journey. But clearly he sees fasting as humbling himself before God and seeking God's help. He ends his report on the episode by saying, 'The hand of our

God was over us, and He delivered us from the hand of the enemy and the ambushes by the way' (Ezra 8:31).

Fasting is also a way of saying, 'This is important.' When God complains about Israel's fasts, He poses the question, 'Is it a fast like this which I choose, a day for a man to *humble* himself? (Isaiah 58:8) He points out that He is not pleased with their fasts because they do it from contention and strife and not out of care for others. If only they had fasted to break the bonds of wickedness, then He would have been pleased. Right in the middle of God's complaint, however, He says, 'You do not fast like you do today to make your voice heard on high.' That should have been their real motive instead of their selfish strife. You may remember the Pharisees were criticised because they fasted so as to be seen by men that they were fasting. They were not really coming with the intention of making their prayers 'heard on high', neither were the people of Isaiah's day. When we fast we are, in effect, stamping our requests: 'Important and urgent'.

Fasting is a means of setting aside other interests in order to seek a knowledge of God's will. Daniel frequently turned to prayer and fasting as he sought to know God's purposes. In Acts 13, we see the five prophets and teachers of the Church in Antioch waiting upon God. Luke records that 'they were ministering to the Lord and fasting.' The word translated 'ministering' literally means 'to perform public service at one's own expense.' These leaders at Antioch were ministering to the Lord 'at their own expense'; in other words they were giving of their own time and going without food. It was during this time that the Holy Spirit said, 'Set apart for Me Barnabas and Saul for the work to which I have called them.' They had taken time to wait upon God, in order to hear His voice, and food certainly wasn't going to stop them in this pursuit. Having discovered the will of God, we read that 'when they had fasted and prayed and laid their hands on them, they sent them away.' Their valediction was celebrated not with a feast but with a fast; how different to our normal practice. Perhaps some of those sent out in our day, to minister in the name of the Lord, would know greater blessing if we commended them to the Lord with prayer and fasting as a mark of our earnest desire to see God's blessing upon them.

Fasting was seen to be a part of normal church life, but today it is such a rarity in most churches and amongst most Christians. Yet Jesus said, 'When you fast . . .' When He was challenged by the Pharisees as to why His disciples did not fast, He replied that while the Bridegroom was present people don't fast, but when he is 'taken away from them, then they will fast' (Matthew 9:15). There is no doubt, therefore, that Jesus saw fasting as a normal Christian activity, and not something for the super-spiritual.

We, as Christians may not find fasting easy, but as we fast and pray, our fasting may be turned to feasting; our mourning to rejoicing. That was the message that the prophet Zechariah gave to a deputation that was sent from the town of Bethel. They wanted to know whether they should fast in the fifth month of the year, as previously. At first, Zechariah did not give them a direct reply but simply brought a question to them from God. 'When you fasted and mourned in the fifth and seventh months these seventy years, was it actually for Me that you fasted? And when you eat and drink, do you not eat for yourselves and do you not drink for yourselves?' (Zechariah 7:5,6). Then God reminds them that they had gone into captivity because of the disobedience of the nation, but now He was restoring them again to the land of Israel and the city of Jerusalem.

Finally, the prophet brings God's direct answer to the question. 'Thus says the Lord of hosts, "The fast of the fourth, the fast of the fifth, the fast of the seventh, and the fast of the tenth months will become joy, gladness, and cheerful feasts for the house of Judah; so love truth and peace" ' (Zechariah 8:19). God goes on to make it plain that people from many cities and even nations would come to the Jews at Jerusalem to seek the favour of the Lord.

What a transformation! For seventy years they had mourned over the destruction of their nation and its capital. They remembered the most disastrous events leading up to their captivity by fasting in the fourth, fifth, seventh and tenth months, yet it seems that they hadn't really been fasting to know the Lord and His purposes. They were bemoaning their lot, rather then genuinely seeking God. Nevertheless, God was going to be gracious and restore them. Now, seventy years on, instead of fasting, they would feast; instead of sorrowing, they would rejoice Now, because God was acting on their behalf, other nations would come to their land seeking the Lord.

What a challenge that is! When we fast, are we really seeking the Lord's interests? Even when our motives are not always pure, God may still be gracious, and restore His blessing. As a result others may well come to seek the favour of the Lord with us. Wouldn't it be good if we, as a nation, so sought God through prayer and fasting that He moved in mighty power upon us so that other nations joined us to seek God's blessing? As a result we might see not only a mighty revival in Britain but also right across the face of the earth. Let's not fast just to grieve over former glories, or the present state of our nation, or even for our blessing, but fast out of a genuine desire to seek God Himself! I have a feeling that if we fasted like that, God would delight in turning our fasts into joyful feasts. We could have some real celebrations then!

15

The Place of Praise

Praise is important in spiritual warfare, but its place has been over-stressed and misunderstood. Many seem to suggest that if we praise God, we defeat the enemy. Such a view, however, is based on very shaky foundations.

The first major misunderstanding comes when people quote from 2 Chronicles 20:22. 'When they began singing and praising, the Lord set ambushes against the sons of Ammon, Moab and Mount Seir . . . so they were routed.' That appears to support the idea that praise is a weapon to defeat the enemy. However, let us examine the situation more closely.

The story begins with Jehoshaphat receiving an intelligence report that a confederation of three armies was marching on Judah. Naturally, the king was filled with fear, but wisely called the nation together to pray and fast. People came from all over the country to plead for God's help. The King led the nation in prayer as men, women and children came to seek the intervention of Almighty God on behalf of their land. There and then, in that day of prayer, the Spirit of God came upon Jahaziel who brought God's prophetic word to them: 'Do not fear or be dismayed because of this great multitude, for the battle is not yours but God's . . . You need not fight in this battle; station yourselves, stand and see the salvation of the Lord on your behalf . . .' As a result of this word from God, they worshipped God and praised Him 'with a very loud voice.'

The next morning Jehoshaphat encouraged the people to

trust in God and His prophetic word. Then he appointed people to go out, before the army, and praise the Lord for His loving kindness. As they began praising, God then set the ambushes, so that the enemy was thrown into confusion. All the Israeli army had to do on that occasion was to collect the spoils of war, which took three whole days.

In analysing the story, we see that this victory was won in answer to prayer. As they called upon God, He not only heard their cry, but gave the prophetic word, assuring them of victory. From that point onwards, the only thing Israel could do was to praise God. Praise not only became an expression of their thanksgiving, but also their faith in God's promise. To say that praise brought about the victory is a complete misunderstanding of the facts.

It seems that many Christians want to avoid the hard graft of fasting and prayer; they want to short-circuit things and move straight to praise as a means of defeating the enemy. When we have prayed and received God's answer, whether it is a prophetic word, or the witness of the Spirit that God has heard our prayers, or the word of authority to bind the enemy, then we can turn to praise, but the work is done in prayer.

If we say that praise defeats the enemy, then everything relies on our effort. The impression is given that if we praise God enough, the enemy will be defeated. That is not so. It is God who acts. Not even prayer produces the change, but God, who acts according to our prayers. Even our prayers have to be brought into harmony with the will and purposes of God.

God chooses and promises to act in response to our prayers, not our praises. When Solomon dedicated the temple, he asked God to hear the prayers of the people, as they gathered in the temple, at times of national crisis such as war, drought, famine, or plague. God's response was that familiar passage of Scripture: 'If I shut the heavens so that there is no rain (etc) . . . and My people who are called by My name humble themselves and pray, and seek My face and turn from their wicked ways, then I will hear from heaven, will forgive their sin, and will heal their land' (2 Chronicles 7:13,14). God promised to respond to their prayers, humility, repentance and fellowship; not their praises, because far more was required than just a celebration time. If they were under judgement, praise could never lift that, but only the conditions already mentioned. It is only repentance and prayer which can begin to restore the nation to blessing.

I believe that Jehoshaphat understood this principle and acted on the basis of the promise given to Solomon. We have already seen in the previous chapter that fasting is linked with humbling oneself. Jehoshaphat, therefore, called the people to prayer and fasting. In his prayer, he remembers the promise linked with the dedication of the temple. He prays: 'They have build Thee a sanctuary there for Thy name, saying, "Should evil come upon us, the sword, on judgement, or pestilence, or famine, we will stand before this house and before Thee (for Thy name is in this house) and cry to Thee in our distress, and Thou wilt hear and deliver us" ' (2 Chronicles 20:8,9). That prayer is a summary of Solomon's prayer and God's response. Jehoshaphat understood then that God would only respond to their repentance and prayer. Praise could not defeat the enemy.

Another passage that is often misused in this matter of praise and spiritual warfare is Psalm 149:6–8. 'Let the high praises of God be in their mouth, and a two-edged sword in their hand, to execute vengeance on the nations, and punishment on the peoples; to bind their kings with chains, and their nobles in fetters of iron.'

The first thing we have to ask ourselves, is it praise or the sword that is used to execute vengeance, punish the people, and to subjugate kings and nobles? While praise is necessary in our warfare, the major weapon used to execute vengeance, in any battle, is the sword.

If we examine the Psalm as a whole, we will see that it encourages people to praise God in a variety of ways. In fact, immediately before the verses quoted above, it says, 'Let them sing for joy on their beds.' Perhaps that should become the latest posture for spiritual warfare! Some Christians would like that excuse. In the first verse it talks about praising the Lord 'in the congregation of the godly one.' The psalmist is saying, in effect, 'Let's praise God in the congregation, even on our beds, and on the battle field.' All of life's situations are to be taken up with praising God.

However, this does bring us to an important issue. When Israel went out to battle, the tribe of Judah led the way. Judah means 'praise'. When we go into battle against our enemy, it is good to praise the Lord; it lifts our eyes up to God. If we fix our attention on the enemy, then our hearts sink, but if we look to God and worship Him for His power, then our expectation begins to rise and we are no longer dejected. The first step to defeat is discouragement. A measure of praise is therefore essential in spiritual warfare.

If we again examine Jehoshaphat's prayer, we see that he begins it by saying, 'O Lord, the God of our fathers, art Thou not God in the heavens? And art Thou not ruler over all the kingdoms of the nations? Power and might are in Thy hand so that no one can stand against Thee.' There is a mixture here of beginning to make his plea to God, but also of praising God for His greatness. It is also worth noting that the praise is directed towards God, not the enemy.

Now to return to Psalm 149; I believe that the Psalmist is showing that the whole of life should be filled with praise. Even when the sword is in our hands, we come with the praise of God in our mouths (literally, in our throats). It almost becomes our war-cry with words like, 'Jesus is Lord!' Spiritual warfare becomes an expression of our worship as we seek to destroy the strongholds of Satan, for we know that to our God belongs worship, honour, dominion and authority. We, therefore, take the sword, with His praise on our lips.

We need to understand clearly, however, that it is prayer which brings the breakthrough against the enemy and not praise. If we examine the Scriptures we see that this is the case. God says, 'If my people pray . . . I will heal their land.' Paul talks about fighting against principalities and powers, and having listed the armour, he stresses the importance of prayer. There is no mention of praise as being a weapon of war. The same is true of Daniel when the angels enter the conflict against the Prince of Persia. He fasted and prayed for three weeks. Later, when he seeks the restoration of the Land, he comes with confession and prayer. Nehemiah, likewise, turns to prayer and fasting over the broken walls of Jerusalem. When Jesus talks about binding and loosing, or removing mountains, it is in the context of prayer. In every one of these cases, it is prayer that brings about the change, not praise. The idea that, somehow, praise defeats the enemy is based on the misuse of a few Scriptures. The word of God is clear that prayer is the means of healing the land, or bind the enemy. We might also add that the sword, mentioned in Psalm 149, which binds the enemy in chains, is the word of God, including the word of authority from God against the enemy.

During Mission England in July, 1984, Billy Graham was speaking in Liverpool. All through that week of meetings, we arranged, in our fellowship, to hold a prayer meeting for those who were not attending the crusade. One night we were led to pray that God would use this campaign to shake the powers of darkness. We prayed that people would be brought out of spiritism, Hinduism, Islam and various occultic practices. We wanted to see the strongholds of Satan shaken. We were even as bold as to ask God for a sign that He had heard us. We don't very often pray along those lines, but this time we did. At approximately eight o'clock the next morning, an earthquake shook Merseyside. Its epicentre was just off the coast of Liverpool and North Wales, but the main impact was in Liverpool itself. Miraculously, although it was a strong quake, no one was injured and there was very little structural damage.

It so happened that our IFB group was due to meet that morning. Just two hours after the earthquake, we gathered together and began to pray about the Dock Strike. (This was the first time that the miners tried to gain the support of dockers.) Already there had been chaos at the Channel ports and especially at Dover. As we prayed, we felt that God had responded to our prayers of the previous night and had shaken Britain loose from the powers of darkness – at least for a temporary period of time. The shock waves of the earthquake had, after all, been felt right across Britain, even to the Channel ports in the east and south. We felt that the Lord was saying to us that morning, 'The battle is mine' as He did to Jehoshaphat. With 2 Chronicles 20 in mind, we prayed that God would bring a similar confusion into the strike situation as God did with Jehoshaphat's opponents. The over-riding feeling was that the victory had really been achieved in the previous night's praying, and that all we really needed to do, that morning, was to praise the Lord for His victory. The prayer meeting consequently became a praise meeting. By nine o'clock that night, news came through that the Dover dockers had returned to work, although the meeting with ACAS had not reached an agreement. A few hours later, the ACAS talks produced a solution, but, in the confusion, dockers in other parts of the country had already started to return. It was an incredible turn of events! (Incidentally, we did hear, later, of Spiritualists, Hindus, and others coming to know the Lord in Liverpool through Mission England.)

About six to eight weeks later, there was another attempt to get the dockers to join with the miners. This became a much more serious threat, with every port in the country being coerced to join the strike. As we prayed at a Prayer and Bible Week, a few ports refused to join the strike. Then somebody suggested that instead of praying, we should use our imaginations, and praise the Lord over every port. The situation that had shown some sign of breaking, suddenly worsened. The next day we turned again to prayer with strong pleading with the Lord. During the course of that day and into the next, the situation improved and within a few days, the strike was over. It was as if God's judgement was hanging over our land. We cannot break the power of the enemy by praise; only God can do that in response to our humble pleading and recognition of the nation's sin. In such a situation, it is wrong to think that we can use praise as a weapon against the enemy, instead of pleading with God for mercy.

I hope that these two examples illustrate the points I have been making. In the first case, it was not praise that changed the situation, but praise arose out of a sense of the victory that God was giving. We didn't even have to bind the enemy on that day because the battle was the Lord's. In the second incident, we mistakenly thought praise would bring victory. It didn't! Only God gives the victory, in response to strong pleading. 'He will call upon Me, and I will answer him,' says God (Psalm 91:15). God's way is still 'If My people who are called by My name humble themselves and pray, and seek My face and turn from their wicked ways, then I will hear from heaven, will forgive their sins, and will heal their land.'

16

Problems of Prayer

One of the dangers of writing a book like this is that we portray all the great successes of prayer and leave people discouraged because their prayer life never comes up to that standard. The illustrations of answered prayer in this book have been included to give examples of how to pray, and not to create the impression that we never have any failures! We need to investigate why we suffer disappointments. Perhaps we can learn more from our failure to get the desired results than from our successes. We must never be afraid to analyse our set-backs; not in a morbid manner but in the confidence that we have a wonderful heavenly Father who is a prayer-answering God.

One of the greatest disappointments we experienced as a Church concerned one of our members who was suffering from cancer. We had prayed for her healing and believed that God would heal. All sorts of words from Scripture were given, by various people in our fellowship, that God was going to heal her. It never happened! She died six days after my parents were killed in a car crash. In some ways the death of this lady was a greater blow than that of my parents. I could come to terms with my parents' death; they had died instantly and together. There was no parting for them as a couple, and no pain, as they were both dead on arrival at the hospital. There were no long years of suffering or failing health or increasing weaknesses. Although they were in their seventies, they had been active to the last moment. They had been one in life and death and in entering into the presence of God, for they knew the Lord. Their transfer from earth to heaven could not have been speedier. What more could one ask if anyone was to lose one's parents? God gave me absolute peace through it all, and I thank God for His goodness.

The news of this sister's death was broken to me as my wife and I walked away from the crematorium to get into the waiting funeral car. That news knocked me for six. My mind went into a spin; what about all those verses people had been given? Where did they come from? One thing was clear; they weren't from God, but where did we go wrong?

I am still not sure of the answer, but the mind can easily conjure up the verses that we want. Our desire can over-rule every word that God might have been speaking. Human emotions can play havoc when trying to hear the voice of God. It was also very easy for us to accept those verses and to feel that, if we did not accept them we were walking in unbelief; if we did not receive them, perhaps our lack of faith would hinder her healing? Consequently, there was the pressure to accept the verses about healing, even if we were unsure that they were relevant here. We had not weighed the matter carefully enough to see if these words were from God, or our own hearts. Maybe we needed a greater maturity to sort out our own desires and hear the voice of God correctly? I believe that this experience was part of the learning process and hopefully we are all the wiser for it.

I am comforted by the fact that Habakkuk seemed to have a similar problem with understanding the purposes of God. It is obvious from the opening words of his book that he had been prayimg for a long time concerning the violence and wickedness in his day. Yet the situation was not getting any better, and it seemed that God wasn't listening.

God's reply was quite simple: 'I am doing something in your days – you would not believe if you were told.' God's answer to the violence in Israel was to bring in the violent Chaldeans to march across their land. This was more than Habakkuk could stand. He protested: 'Why are you silent when the wicked swallowed up those more righteous than they? . . . Will they (the Chaldeans) therefore empty their net and continually slay nations without sparing?'

God's reply was simple and to the point: 'The vision is yet for the appointed time; it hastens towards the goal, and it will not fail. Though it tarries, wait for it; for it will certainly come, it will not delay.' It was plain, then, that God's judgement would come and Judah would be conquered.

By the end of the book Habakkuk has come to accept God's word, and although he hates what he hears, he knows he must trust in God. He sees the signs of the devastation to come and says:

'Though the fig tree should not blossom,
And there be no fruit on the vines,
Though the yield of the olive should fail,
And the fields produce no food,
Though the flock should be cut off from the fold,
And there be no cattle in the stalls,
Yet I will exult in the Lord,
I will rejoice in the God of my salvation.
The Lord God is my strength,
And He has made my feet like hinds' feet,
And makes me walk on my high places.'

It was a struggle for Habakkuk to bring his desires into conformity with the will of God, but he began to understand what God was doing. You may remember we have already noted that John says, 'If we ask anything according to His will, He hears us' (1 John 5:14). There may come a day when Britain will be so ripe for judgement that we shall have to face the same struggle as Habakkuk and rejoice in the God of our salvation, although destruction is coming upon the land. May God save us from that! I believe that at the moment God is showing us mercy, although we are under a measure of His judgement. We need to pray that God will go on being merciful and that, in our case, the tide of wickedness and violence can be turned back, if God's people pray.

One very simple problem with which most Christians struggle whilst praying, is that of wandering thoughts. Other matters often press upon our mind. The psalmist said, 'I was crying to the Lord with my voice' (Psalm 3:4). It may well have been his distress that caused him to pray in such a manner, but speaking aloud is one way to concentrate when praying. Sometimes we may need to pray about those things that are dominating our thoughts before we can pray about other matters. At other times, we have to exercise some real discipline and press on by praying out aloud to help our concentration.

I think most Christians also assume that God automatically hears our prayers and answers them, but scripture says, 'If I regard wickedness in my heart, the Lord will not hear' (Psalm 66:18). It is clear from this verse that when we allow sin to go unchecked and unconfessed in our lives, then it becomes a barrier to our prayers even being heard. There are other passages in the Old Testament that make the same point. Proverbs 28:9 says, 'He who turns away his ear from listening to the law, even his prayer is an abomination.' That was part of Israel's trouble; so much so that God said through Isaiah, 'When you spread out your hands in prayer, I will hide My eyes from you, yes, even though you multiply prayers, I will not listen' (Isaiah 1:15).

We find the same emphasis in the New Testament. John, for example, tells us that 'If our heart does not condemn us, we have confidence before God; and whatever we ask we receive from Him, because we keep His commandments and do the things that are pleasing in His sight' (1 John 3:21,22). That obviously implies that if we are disobeying God, and our hearts condemn us, then we can have no confidence that God will hear us. When our hearts do condemn us, then we need to confess our sin, return to obedience, and expect God to begin to hear us again.

In this connection, we need to remember that Jesus told us that when we pray, we need to forgive people. If we are holding on to bitterness, or resentment against others, then that becomes a barrier to our prayers. It is 'regarding iniquity in our hearts.'

114

God also considers the matter of relationships as being important; for instance, Peter makes it plain that if husbands are not treating their wives properly their prayers will be hindered (see 1 Peter 3:7). It may also relate to Peter's statement on wives being properly in submission to their husbands. Malachi makes a similar point in saying that God has not accepted the sacrifices of some men, because they had broken faith with their wives regarding their marriage covenant (Malachi 2:13,14).

We are so concerned about getting our requests answered, but God is more concerned about us being the holy people He called us to be. We forget the statement of James that 'the prayer of a righteous man is powerful and effective' (James 5:16 NIV). It is almost as if God disciplines us by saying, 'You are asking Me to do this for you, but you haven't listened for a moment to what I have been saying. First get your life right, then I will listen.'

The danger of referring to verses like those quoted is that some people will immediately feel that their prayers have not been answered because of some sin, somewhere, that has not been confessed. Satan would easily bring us under condemnation, but it may be, like Habakkuk, that we haven't understood the purposes of God, or that God's timing is different to ours.

One familiar phrase repeated in Scriptures is, 'How long?' David asks that question four times in Psalm 13 alone. 'How long will my enemy be exalted over me?', he asks among the other questions. The Israelites must have asked that question many times when suffering slavery in Egypt. It is quite clear from the Exodus account that God heard their cries, but He was preparing His man in the wilderness of Sinai. I wonder how many other men God has prepared in a wilderness situation? The trouble is, we want quick results. God's delays often prove essential, even for our prayers to be answered.

We, as a church, were trying to buy a house that had been unoccupied for several years. The owner, who was an elderly lady, agreed to sell, but she failed to complete the necessary forms authorising her solicitor to act. We couldn't understand the delay. Then we, as a fellowship, were led out of the denominational set-up in which we were involved. The trust deed of the buildings and the church prevented us from operating on a biblical basis as far as eldership and Church government were concerned. It meant we had to forfeit our premises. Almost as soon as we left the premises, we saw some progress on purchasing the house and within six months of leaving the church buildings, the house was ours! We realised then what a blessing the delay had proved to be! If we had bought the house when we wished, it would have been linked with the trust deed of the church, and we would have had to forfeit the very house we had bought. God answers our prayers in His time, which is always best.

Perhaps the biggest problem regarding prayer is this matter of delay. Sometimes we wonder whether God is not answering our prayers, either because He has a different purpose to us, or because of sin in our lives – yet again and again, God has heard us, but He has not been in the same hurry. He is a God of infinite patience and measures everything against the perspective of eternity. For Abraham and Sarah, God's delay was unbearable. As a result, they came up with their own solution, involving Hagar, producing a son who had been fathered by Abraham. Yet the birth of their own son, when it came, left them laughing with the incredulity of the miracle, as Isaac's name (he laughs) implies.

Mary, the sister of Lazarus, complained about Jesus' delay in responding to her call. It had been a very costly delay, for she complained, 'If you had been here, my brother would not have died.' Yet it is obvious from the account that Jesus had deliberately delayed, so that a greater miracle would result; resurrection rather than healing. It also enabled Him to teach that believers in Him would be raised to life. The delay proved a mighty blessing.

There is just one other matter we need to consider in this chapter. James says, 'You ask and do not receive, because you ask with wrong motives, so that you may spend it on your pleasures' (James 4:3). There is nothing wrong in praying for ourselves, but our motives are important. God does not encourage selfishness. We forget that when we responded to the call of Christ, we were called to deny ourselves and take up our cross in order to die to self. It's a pity we resurrect the old ego so quickly. God will not encourage us to do so, and therefore refuses to answer selfish prayer. That is not to say God does not sometimes delight in giving us some luxury from time to time, but He will not indulge our fleshly appetites.

We, like Paul, find ourselves puzzled by unanswered prayer. At times, we have to endure some 'thorn in the flesh' (those prickly attacks from the enemy) instead of having it removed. God chooses to grant the grace with which to overcome the problems, rather than remove them. God will not treat us as members of the kindergarten all our lives, but as men and women of maturity who reflect the glory of God in their problems. That becomes a greater testimony to His power and trains us for service in a way that nothing else could. We need a bit more backbone in our Christianity than is often seen in the Church.

These are some of the problems that we have in understanding prayer. We want instant answers; God wants fellowship and obedience. We want success and sensationalism; God wants sanctification. We want an easy way out; God wants maturity. All of this is costly in time and devotion, especially in knowing the purposes of God. At the end of it all, however, we shall be much nearer to producing those prayers of a righteous man that are powerful and effective.

17

A Land Not Rained On

God spoke to Ezekiel saying, 'Son of man, say to her (the house of Israel), "You are a land that is not cleansed or rained on in the day of indignation." ' God then continues by condemning the priests, prophets, princes and people for their sin. Consequently as a nation they are ripe for judgement. God concludes the message by declaring that He has been looking for someone to stand in the gap, so that He might turn away from His anger and judgement.

As a nation, we deserve God's judgement. We have polluted the land with adultery and abortions, pornography and promiscuity, murder and violence, spiritism and witchcraft, sorcery and sodomy. What a contrast to the past when we, as a nation, took the gospel to the world? We, who have such a rich Christian heritage, are now neglecting God's Word. The Church has distorted the Word of God and rejected the truth. Are we not ripe for judgement? I tell you we are!

Yet I have one reason for hope. I find that God is raising up a groundswell of intercession. There are many other groups, apart from IFB, that are praying for our nation and I thank God for every one of them. God cannot say of Britain that there is no one to stand in the gap, although we may be lacking people with the quality and persistence of Moses. We need to plead with God for our nation, because our sins have multiplied to an alarming degree. Almost weekly, we discover that we have gone down the slippery slope a little further into degradation and rebellion against God. We are already suffering a measure of God's judgement in that He has given our nation over to a spiritual malaise, false religions, the occult and increasing crime, yet it may not be too late to save our nation. I find encouragement because God is always looking for those standing in the gap as a way of turning back from His anger. My prayer is that this book will cause many others to stand in the gap and call upon God for mercy.

I believe that God is even now looking for a way to bless our land. At the Prayer and Bible Week held in Manchester during the year of the drought (1976), when those who were gathered there confessed the sins of the Church, then and only then, could they begin to ask God to send rain. They asked God to send the rain only if He was willing to send the rain of His Spirit. Before the week was out, after months and months of unbelievably dry weather, without any rain, it poured all over the nation – and we had one of the wettest winters! In months, the empty reservoirs were filled. The water authorities had said it would take two wet winters and a summer before they could possibly be full again. God did it in a matter of months. I believe God expressed His heart in that He was willing to send the latter rain of His Spirit. Now let us express our hearts and plead for the outpouring of His Spirit!

England is a land that has not been 'cleansed or rained on' since the time of the Wesleyan revival. There have been revivals in Ulster, Wales, and more recently in the Hebrides, but England has seen nothing since Wesley. At that time God so poured out His Spirit that Wesley could preach to miners before they went down the pits and hundreds were converted. Thousands at the time of Wesley were swept into the Kingdom in that revival tide. Churches sprang up all over the land to accommodate the converts.

It has been said by various historians that Britain was saved from a bloody revolution, such as was experienced by France, because of the Wesleyan revival. Britain again needs a mighty move of God's Spirit to change men's hearts. With so much wickedness in our nation, we need our land to be cleansed and rained on.

The 1859 revival in Ulster brought some interesting statistics on crime. There had been a gradual drop in the number of criminal convictions in the few years before the main revival, but in the five years from 1855–60 the criminal convictions per annum had virtually halved in the six counties.[1]

It is very clear that, at the present time, with prisons near to bursting point in the British isles, we could well do with a similar breath of the Spirit to move across our land. We have had such a decline in moral standards that a third of all youths between the ages of 17 and 25 years have a criminal record, according to Home Office statistics. Shoplifting and stealing from one's place of employment have reached almost epidemic proportions. There is also a vast increase in violence, murder and rape. When we lose respect for God, we soon lose respect for people and property.

The 1904 Welsh revivals meant that hymns used to echo through the valleys and in the pits. Gone are those days. Many of the chapels that are scattered so prolifically throughout Wales are now simply monuments to a past move of God. Wales like the rest of the United Kingdom needs a fresh move of God's Spirit. It's amazing how quickly the effects of revival are lost. We are told that the Israelites followed the Lord during the days of Joshua and the other elders who had seen the great work God did. Then 'there arose another generation after them who did not know the Lord' (Judges 2:10).

Scotland was partially touched by the 1859 revival which resulted in a 10% increase in church membership. While church attendance in Scotland is probably better than England, it again needs the Spirit of God to breathe fresh life upon it.

Right in the middle of a word spoken to Cyrus the Persian, there is this plea: 'Drip down, O heavens, from above, and let the clouds pour down righteousness; let the earth open up and salvation bear fruit, and righteousness spring up with it' (Isaiah 45:8). When God's Spirit is poured

[1]889 to 456 convictions, p. 179 *The Second Evangelical Awakening in Britain* Dr Edwin Orr.

out upon the land, then there comes forth a new righteousness, for God's Spirit convicts of sin. That was obvious in the Ulster Revival of 1859, and it has been seen again and again as people, under conviction, have paid debts to shopkeepers, returned stolen goods, and admitted crimes to the police. Higher standards of morality were also restored. No wonder God described Israel (through Ezekiel) as a land that had not been cleansed or rained on. When the rain comes it washes the dirt from the streets. When God's Spirit comes it cleanses the land of its moral pollution.

From the verse in Isaiah 45 we can see how salvation comes. The Spirit 'drips down' from heaven, but earth sees the fruit of salvation. Isn't that true? Salvation does not come from man's own activity, but being born from above and being born again of the Holy Spirit. When God's Spirit is poured out, more is achieved in a few months of revival than years of evangelism. The day of Pentecost saw 3,000 being saved just in Jerusalem. We need God's Spirit to be poured out upon Britain at this time, if we are going to see a real turning to God.

Zechariah 10 is a very interesting chapter. It says 'Ask rain from the Lord at the time of the latter rain.' In Israel the latter rain comes in the Spring. The former rain starts in October or November, but it is the latter rain that helps to swell the grain of barley harvest at Pentecost. (Pentecost is the Jews' early harvest festival.) Without that rain, there would be a limited harvest. The prophet talks about God who sends the storm clouds. Spring time in Israel is the time of thunder storms that drench the land.

While it is clear that Zechariah is talking about the natural rain and the vegetation in the field, he suddenly adds, 'for the teraphim speak iniquity, and the diviners see lying visions.' He continues by talking about the Lord visiting his flock, the house of Judah, and strengthening it like a war horse, and saving the house of Judah. What is the connection between this and the rain?

It seems that the prophet could not divorce the natural rain from the spiritual rain. The Israelites needed to ask for storms so that there would be a full harvest, but they needed to ask for the rain of God's Spirit because of all the occultic practices of the idolaters and diviners. The Spirit would also revive the house of Judah. The Holy Spirit was the only answer to Satan's activity, and to reviving God's people.

During the year of the great drought, we saw a land that was parched, as we have never seen it before. I remember seeing cabbages in Bedfordshire that were stunted, shrivelled and dying. Some had scarcely grown since the day they were planted. It was pathetic! As we prayed for God to send the rain, we began to realise that what we saw in nature was true of Britain, spiritually; it was dry, barren and dying. We could no longer just pray for rain; it had to be also the rain of God's Spirit. Obviously, Zechariah saw it like that too.

The rain that Zechariah spoke about would revive Judah, turn her from her sorceries, save her and strengthen her. Isn't that what God's Spirit does? The coming of the Spirit at Pentecost turned a frightened church into a strong witnessing people, with thousands being saved. I believe those words of Zechariah have a special significance for our day.

James also talks about the latter rain when he writes: 'Be patient, therefore, brethren until the coming of the Lord. Behold the farmer waits for the precious produce of the soil, being patient about it, until it gets the early and late rains' (James 5:7). It is as if he is saying that they had the early rain at Pentecost, but before the Lord returns, they needed the later rain. A farmer waited for that rain for a bumper harvest, and the Church of God must equally wait for the late rains.

If we put these two verses together from James and Zechariah, then we have two important lessons to learn. The first, is that Israel will know a time of spiritual renewal just before the return of Jesus. Paul quite clearly states that will happen. He says, 'A partial hardening has happened to Israel until the fulness of the Gentiles has come in; and thus all Israel will be saved; just as it is written, 'The deliverer will come from Zion, He will remove ungodliness from *Jacob* (Israel). And this is My covenant with them, when I take away their sins.' He then goes on to say that from the standpoint of the gospel the Jews are enemies, but from God's standpoint they are beloved for the fathers' sake (Abraham, Isaac and Jacob) and that God's calling is irrevocable. Earlier he has talked about how their rejection of Jesus brought reconciliation to the world, but their acceptance would bring life from the dead. We wait such a move of God upon Jewish people.

Zechariah also mentions a move of God's Spirit: 'I will pour out on the house of David and on the inhabitants of Jerusalem, the Spirit of grace and of supplication, so that they will look on Me whom they have pierced; and they will mourn for Him, as one mourns for an only son, and they will weep bitterly over Him, like the bitter weeping over a first-born.' He says that the mourning will be like the mourning of Hadadrimmon in the plain of Megiddo. This is usually considered to be a reference to the death of King Josiah who was one of Judah's most popular kings. In other words, Zechariah is saying that the house of David will experience a time of national mourning over Jesus whom they pierced. Israel has never come to that position.

It is interesting that this time of mourning is prophesied just 2 chapters after the prophet's command to pray for rain in the time of latter rain. Zechariah follows his prophecy of national mourning by saying that a 'fountain will be opened for the house of David and for the inhabitants of Jerusalem, for sin and impurity' (13:1). Just one chapter later he states that the feet of the Lord will stand on the Mount of Olives (14.4). As Jesus ascended from the Mount of Olives the angel said He would come again in like manner. If we summarise those closing chapters of Zechariah, he shows the need to pray for God's Spirit, that idolatry and occultism might be washed away and the house of David revived. Then he tells us that as a result of 'the Spirit of grace and supplication' Israel will repent and be cleansed, and finally see Jesus return. Didn't Jesus say to His own people, and especially to Jerusalem: 'Behold I leave your house desolate! For I say to you, from now on you shall not see Me until you say, "Blessed is He who comes in the name of the Lord" '? (Matthew 23:38,39).

The second important lesson we learn from James and Zechariah is that God is wanting not only to save Israel, but to pour His Spirit upon all flesh. Have the words of Joel been completely fulfilled when he declared that God would pour His Spirit on all flesh 'in the last days'? Is there not a latter rain, as well as the former rain, when God will drench the nations? Doesn't God want to save men and women from the various nations where Islam, Communism, Hinduism, Buddhism and Animism holds sway? We need to pray for the rain of God's Spirit upon all flesh. Pentecost only saw it on Jewish flesh.

We have already seen how in Korea there has been a mighty move of God's Spirit. The Church has learnt to engage in prayer and defeat the powers of darkness. Through its pleadings, God has been gracious to visit that nation. We need, as Christians, to confess our sin, the sin of the church, and the nation so that 'times of refreshing may come from the presence of the Lord' (Acts 3:19).

It is good to discover a greater emphasis on prayer, at the present time, within our nation. I find further encouragement in that God has been reviving the Church and putting the power of His Spirit into individual lives and many fellowships and churches up and down the country. God hasn't given up on us by any means, but unless the Church stops looking for spiritual kicks and takes up its cross afresh, being willing to die to all that panders to the flesh, and puts to death any self-seeking, empire-building, jealousy and pride, then we will still miss most of what God has for us. We need to put a fresh emphasis on prayer, together with the rediscovery of the gifts of the Spirit, power for witness and the call to Holy living. We are not invited to a ball, but warfare, and to call upon Almighty God.

This book is dedicated to that end. My prayer is that the Church in Britain will really stand in the gap, and beseech God for an outpouring of His Spirit that will bring thousands into the Kingdom and help prepare the Bride of Christ for His return. I believe God is wanting to pour out His Spirit, but He says, 'If my people pray . . .' God waits for your response; our nation needs your prayers. Britain can know a mighty revival; are God's people ready to pay the price in humble, fervent and persistent prayer? Eternity will tell!

Joel twice declares: 'Blow the trumpet!' The first refers to an alarm, warning of danger. The second relates to a call to prayer and fasting so that God may hear their pleas, and actually send blessing instead of judgement. He suggests that if this is done, God will restore the land, and even pour out His Spirit.

Scripture also shows that the trumpet is sounded as a call to warfare. There is a mixture of all three in this book. There is the warning of judgement if we do not humble ourselves and pray. There is also a clear call to prayer. Perhaps most of all it is a call to warfare. Let us, therefore, rise up and pour out our hearts in seeking the outpouring of God's Spirit upon our land. Let us rise up, too, in spiritual warfare, and seek to win the nation back to God. The trumpet has sounded! Rise up, attack, and take the land for God!

Intercessors for Britain

'If my people who are called by my name humble themselves and pray, and seek my face, and turn from their wicked ways, then I will hear from heaven, and will forgive their sin and heal their land.'

2 Chronicles 7 v 14.

Jesus said:–

'Could you not watch with me one hour?'

At the beginning of 1969, Denis Clark was led to seek 168 intercessors who would pray for one hour a week. With each taking a different hour in the week, an unbroken chain of prayer for Britain would result covering the whole year. Actually, over 200 responded and the numbers have continued to rise and now number several thousand.

Convenant to Pray

We ask those who become part of our prayer fellowship to convenant to pray for one hour a week. We are all full of good intentions, but often we fail to turn that into action. A promise to God therefore means that we have made a commitment which we intend to keep.

Paul made a vow to God on at least two occasions in the

Acts and the Old Testament is full of those who made vows to God and were blessed. The Psalmist says: 'Offer to God a sacrifice of thanksgiving, and pay your vows to the Most High; and call upon Me in the day of trouble; I shall rescue you, and you will honour Me.' (Ps 50: 14, 15) Surely such a commitment to pray is not only a sacrifice of time but a way of seeking to honour God with our devotion. As our land is changed through our intercession that will bring further honour to God.

Your Decision

Do you believe that your prayers along with others could change our nation? Then join the battle for Britain today and send your convenant card, or send for one to:–

> **Intercessors for Britain**
> **14, Orchard Road, Moreton**
> **Wirral, Merseyside, L46 8TS**